Here to Stay

Training Your Rescu

Lily Clark

ISBN 978-1-5272-1953-3

www.suppawt.com

Limits of Liability and Disclaimer of Warranty:

The author shall not be liable in the event of incidental or consequential damages in connection with, or arising out of the instructions and suggestions contained in this book.

For information about wholesale discount for rescues, please contact:

www.dog-and-bone.co.uk

Foreword by Dr. Ian Dunbar

I'll keep this really short because I want you to start reading the book and training your new dog right away.

I JUST ABSOLUTELY LOVE THIS BOOK!

Here to Stay cuts to the chase and gives new dog owners exactly what they need right from the "get go". There's no preamble, waffle, acronyms, complicated terminology, or psychobabble but instead, oodles of important How-To advice. As Lily says, "Ready, Steady Go" and then off we go, as the first few pages outline precisely what to do with your new Rescue Dog on the very 1st Day at Home. The first few days and weeks in a new home are so important because during this time of transition, the dog can most easily learn new household rules and basic manners. It is so refreshing that the urgent and really important information is right up front and not camouflaged by other equally important but much less urgent concepts that are included but come later.

Here to Stay is really well written in a casual and affable, yet very concise and precise style. The concept and layout are just as wonderful as they are whimsical, making the book easy and enjoyable to read and understand. Such important information: Learning how to train your dog — easily, quickly, effectively and enjoyably — is going to change your dog's quality of life … for life! What a lucky dog you have. And in turn, your new dog will change your life.

Here to Stay is going to help so many people and dogs. The book was written especially for people like you, who have just adopted a Rescue dog — a dog that deserves a second chance. Indeed, this book should be mandatory reading. When people leave a Rescue, they should have a new dog and this book! Every Rescue should stock Here To Stay. Moreover, all prospective puppy buyers should read this book too, so that their pups get a decent first chance at a stellar education and so get to stay in their original homes with their original human companions and have no need for a "second chance".

Thank you for buying this book. I very much hope your dog comes, sits and stays awhile with you. Please give your dog a hug from me and please spread the word about Here to Stay.

Well done Lily. Brilliant job. Here to Stay Rocks!

Dr. Ian Dunbar

Berkeley, California

Let the Fun Begin!

Hello! My name is Lily and I will be your guide during your new journey for you and your rescue dog. My passion is to help you communicate effectively and build a long lasting partnership, whilst focusing on the fast and furious rehabilitation of your rescue dog.

Jasper, the star of the book

You have done a wonderful thing bringing an unloved dog into your home and I am going to do my best to make it easier for you. There may be times when you think "Oh no what have I done!" this is completely normal, take a deep breath, have a cup of tea and reanalyse. Your new dog won't believe their luck!

Ready? Set? Go!

Contents

Reactivity

Choosing a Rescue Dog

Well done for choosing to rescue! Before you set off to take a look, make a list of priorities that you would like from the dog. This will prevent you being sucked in by the dog with the sad eyes, which may be the wrong dog for you.

Toilet Trained	Basic Manners	Sociable with dogs	Sociable with people	....
		✓	✓	

What to expect from the rescue:

- Medical log up to date, including neutering, vaccinations and microchip.
- Behavioural log on what the dog knows, any history, what needs more work and how to do this.
- Willingly lets you see the dog interact with all types of people and dogs, including your family.
- Willing to let you walk the dog offsite.
- Multiple visits and home check.
- Ongoing support after homing.

If you choose a dog that is fearful, shy or reactive, set yourself realistic expectations. This is not a companion, this is a project dog.

1st Day at Home

This is an extremely exciting day for all involved, but try and stick to your normal routine so that the dog can begin to adjust. First impressions count and can be critical for success.

Step By Step Guide

Step 1- Set the dog up for success, remove access to anything you don't want the dog to chew or play with. If the dog is unsupervised, confine them to a crate, pen or room where they cannot get into mischief.

Step 2- When the dog first arrives home take them to the toilet area, reward them with treats and praise if they use it, we want this to be a memorable moment (See page 31).

Step 3- Settle them down on their designated bed with a stuffed KONG or chew toy (See page 11).

Step 4- Do not give any commands, but reward anything you like that the dog is doing. This means the dog does not get frustrated if you are asking for behaviours they don't understand, but realise what behaviours pay off i.e. laying quietly chewing a Kong (see page 13).

Step 5- Put into place your house and garden rules and stick to them. I.e. is the dog allowed on the furniture? It's not fair to the dog to keep changing the rules.

Rewards

Rewarding our dogs for doing things we like means they will do these things more often as they pay off! This is called positive reinforcement. Think about what your individual dog finds rewarding, this can depend on their temperament and breed. You may not be able to motivate a dog with toys if they find food more rewarding. Write a list of rewards your dog enjoys and rate them, each reward should complement the aim of the activity.

The way you deliver the reward also affects how rewarding it is: the amount of energy you put into playing with a toy or whether you hand feed or throw the treat. Now you can use different rewards to communicate to your dog how well they have done! Try using some of your dog's daily food allowance for training, as it enriches their day and doesn't add extra calories. Remember when using food as a reward that scent is the most important aspect of the value to the dog, so you can enhance your kibble with other smelly foods to increase the value.

Diet

It is extremely important that your dog has the best rated food in your price range. If you are feeding kibble with lots of fillers and E numbers it will show in your dog's behaviour! Similarly, if you feed children lots of fast food they end up practically bouncing off the walls.

Many dog food sites allow you to input in your dogs' details and budget to find the best food suited to you and your life style. Break your dog's ration down into multiple, small meals for easy digestibility.

A good diet should:

- Make the coat shiny.
- Keep teeth clean and breath fresh.
- Make stools small and firm
- Produce very little gas.
- Balance energy levels.

Ditch the bowl, train or feed your dogs in new and innovative ways and see how much fun they have!

The Power of KONGs- Get Stuffing!

KONGs are bouncy, strong, durable and brilliant! A good and tasty KONG recipe that takes the dog ages to empty, can be used to:

- Help teach dogs to settle.
- Get used to new environments.
- Distract them in stressful situations.
- Keep them occupied.
- Slow down their eating.
- Help in preventing separation anxiety.
- Redirect chewing.

Licking is a comforting and stress relieving behaviour, which makes the KONG great for redirecting stress and frustration onto a suitable activity.

<u>KONG fillings:</u>

- Kibble (dry or soaked) and wet food
- Creamy cheese/normal cheese
- Peanut butter (without Xylitol!)
- Meat and fish patties
- Cooked: brown rice and sweet potatoes
- Natural yogurt

- Honey
- Egg
- Meat
- Vegetables: Broccoli, carrot, peas.
- Fruit: banana, apple, mango.

Tailor the Kong to the diet and needs of your dog.

Easy: For a dog that has not used a KONG before. Start with loosely compacted food which may fall out. Plug the end with something sticky.

Medium: Pack food in tightly; you could soak kibble or mix with something sticky! Pack the end.

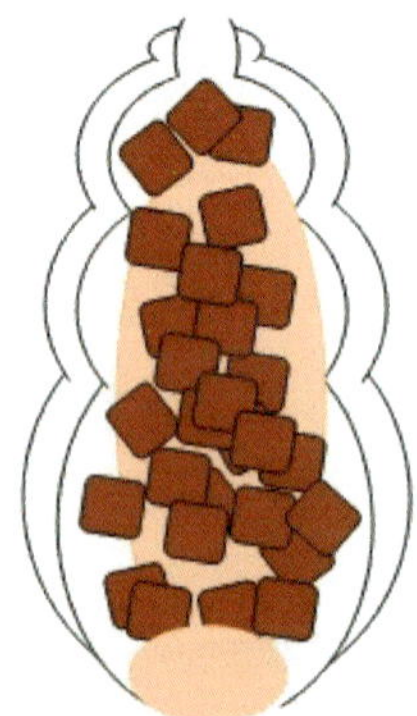

Hard: Freeze or microwave the contents, making it hard or sticky to get out and pack the end. This keeps dogs busy for longer.

All or None

All or None training is simple, easy and extremely effective, no commands are given and the dog is less likely to get frustrated or confused. You simply praise and reward any behaviour you like, to increase the likelihood of the dog displaying that behaviour again. This allows you to pay attention to the good rather than focusing on and giving attention to the 'bad'.

Behaviours you want to encourage:

Example 1- Eliminating in the designated toilet spot.

Example 2- Laying down quietly and relaxing.

Example 3- Routinely checking in with you.

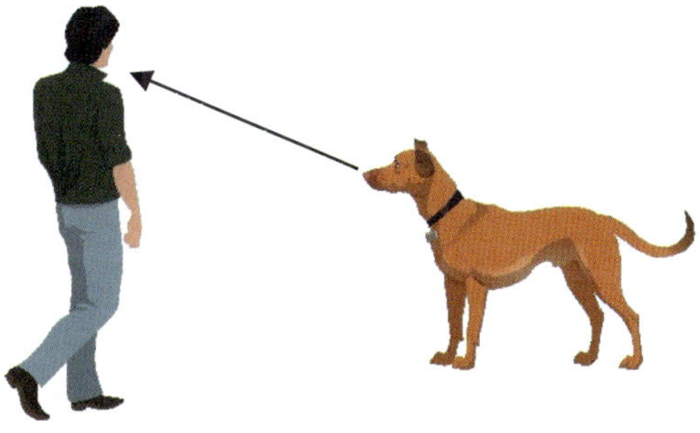

Luring

Luring is the easiest training strategy, used to guide dogs into the position we want, without physically manipulating them. It allows us to easily show the dog what we want and reward the behaviour that we wish to see more of.

Step By Step Guide:

Sit

Step 1- Get the dog's attention with a treat, put the treat near the end of their nose and guide it over the top of their head. This will encourage them to look up which means their bottom will go down. Praise and reward.

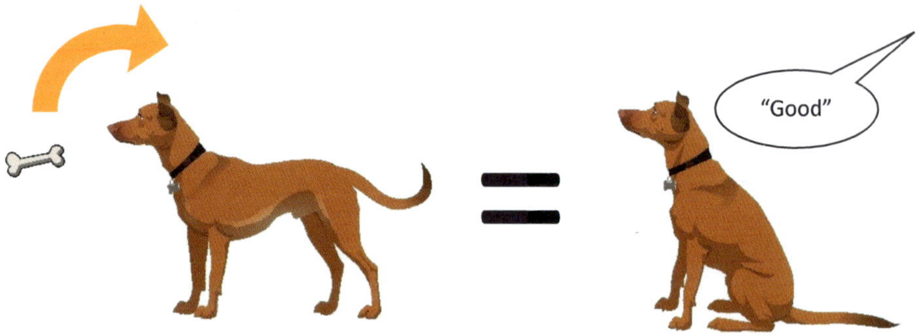

Step 2- After a few repetitions, do this with a pretend treat in your hand. We want the dog to follow our hand movement as this will later become a visual cue. The dog will begin to understand that they will still be rewarded after the behaviour even if the treat is not on display.

Step 3- Once the dog is following the visual cue 90% of the time we can introduce a voice cue. "Sit" followed by a pause and then the hand cue. The dog will begin to associate the word with the handcue.

Down

(Follow steps 2 and 3 from luring sit)

Top Tip: If their bottom pops up continuously, try luring under your leg.

Stand

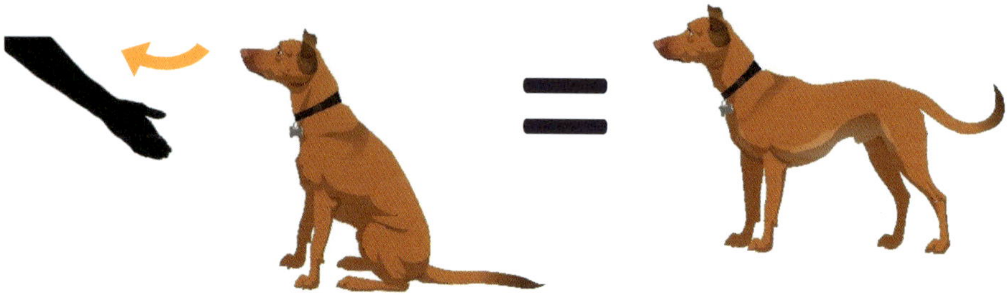

(Follow steps 2 and 3 from luring sit)

Try these as a sequence and reward at the end: Sit, down, stand, down, sit, stand, sit.

Top Tip: Once the dog understands the activity, we need to stop having food in our hands. We teach them to follow our hand signal instead of the food but they still get rewarded. If they will only exhibit the behaviour when you have food in hand you are no longer luring, you are bribing.

Luring Tricks

Teaching your dog tricks is not only fun but very important to keep their brain active. It also strengthens your ability to communicate with your dog effectively. Tricks can be useful, such as rolling over to show their belly to the vet, opening their mouth to have their teeth cleaned, exercising particular muscles and bowing on cue to help initiate play with another dog.

Spin

Bow

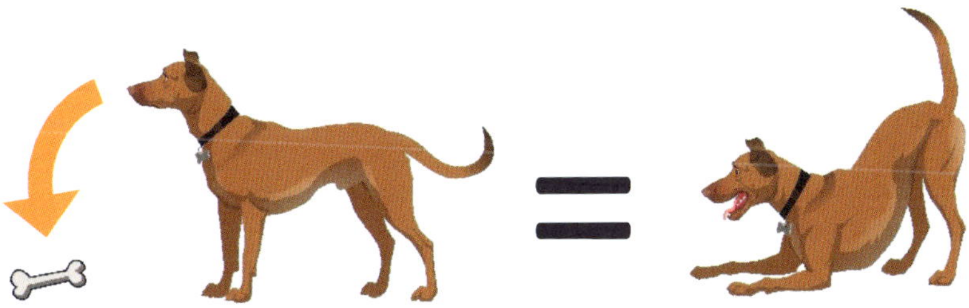

Life Skills

Crate Training

Once a dog has become accustomed to their crate, this quickly becomes their safe place. It provides them with somewhere comfortable to retreat to if they need peace and quiet. A crate also allows us to keep the dog safe and out of harm's way whilst their training plan is underway.

Step By Step Guide

Step 1- Praise and reward the dog for approaching and sniffing the crate. This will encourage the dog to continue this action, in order to be reinforced.

Step 2- Make a fuss of dropping some treats through the top of the crate when the door is shut. The dog will want to eat these. Open the door and let the dog in to retrieve them.

Step 3- Encourage the dog to go in and out of the crate by throwing a treat inside and saying "bed" and then encouraging the dog back out WITHOUT a reward. Soon they will prefer to stay in the crate as this is where the treats are given!

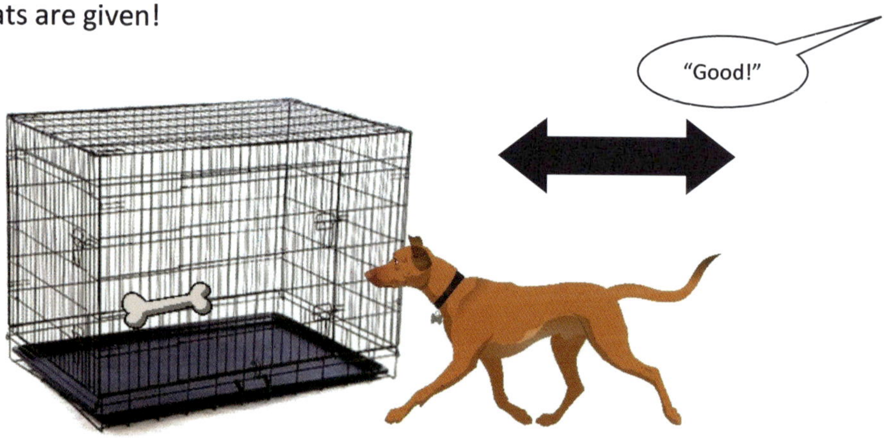

Step 4- Once they are happy going into their crate, give them something to chew which they will engage with whilst being in their crate. Stay in close proximity to the crate to ensure the dog is happy and settled.

Step 5- Repeat step 4, slowly extending the time in their crate. You may begin shutting the crate door when you give them a chew. Wait for 10 seconds of quiet after they have finished their chew to let them out.

Step 6- Pop the dog in their crate with a chew, shut the door and QUIETLY leave. To begin with, only leave for 2 minutes and return before they finish their chew. Slowly build on the time you leave them, ensuring you tailor this to the individual needs of the dog.

Step 7- If they take themselves into the crate of their own accord, reward and praise them highly. We want the dog to associate their crate with positive experiences.

Top Tips:

- Tailor the experience to each dog's individual needs and requirements. If needed, take the process back a few steps.
- Do not rush the process, use the crate for punishment or force the dog inside. These things may cause additional problems.
- Place a blanket over the top of the crate for additional security during times of stress.

Settle Mat

Teaching your dog to settle when needed is a very helpful skill. Teaching it in relation to a specific mat or bed also means you can make your settle portable and take it with you. It can also help with the duration aspect of your stay (see page 36) and give your dog a secure base when guests come to visit.

Step By Step Guide

Step 1- Ask your dog to wait whilst you place a treat on the mat. Use "bed" or "mat" as your release cue for the dog to go and get the treat.

Step 2- Repeat step 1 three times. On the fourth time pretend to place a treat on the mat. When you release them, they will go over to the mat. Praise and reward contact with the mat.

Step 3- Repeat until the dog understands to go and get on their mat on cue. We can now encourage the dog to go to their mat and start to settle by asking for a down.

Step 4- We need to solidify this 'settle' by rewarding them for relaxed behaviour. We also need to bring in distance, duration and distraction as we do when teaching a stay (see page 36).

If your dog goes to the matt and settles of their own accord, give them a 'Jackpot' by rewarding them with lots of treats.

Self-Control Exercise

Self-control is something that we have to teach our dogs. Like a muscle, the more self-control is exercised the better it gets. Dogs love to solve puzzles and this exercise allows the dog to figure out what they need to do in order to get the treats. It also builds an amazing foundation for teaching leave.

Step By Step Guide

Step 1- Put a handful of kibble in your palm and close your hand into a fist around it.

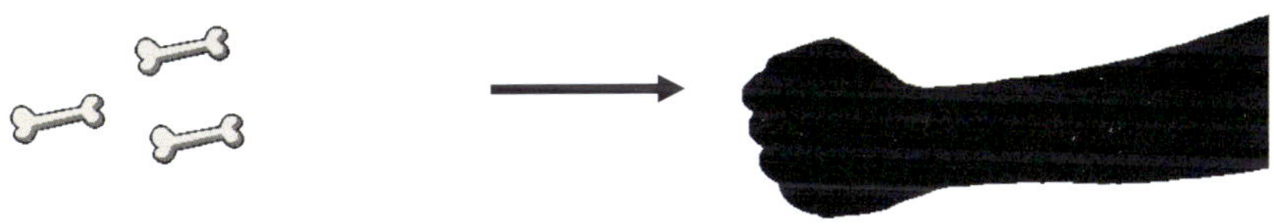

Step 2- The dog will fuss over your hand trying to get the kibble out.

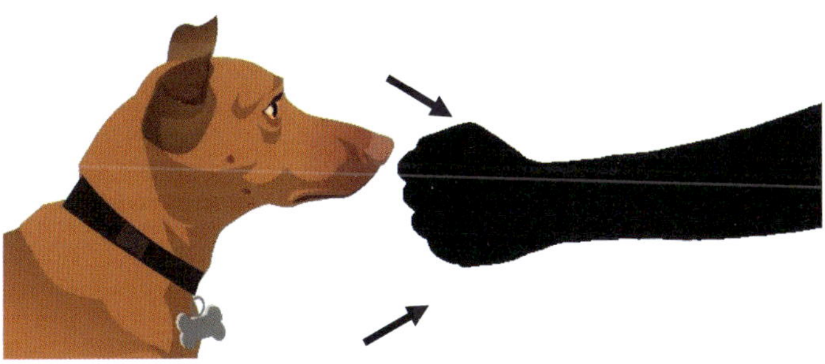

Step 3- As soon as the dog stops fussing for a second, open your hand. *Be ready to shut it if they dive back in!*

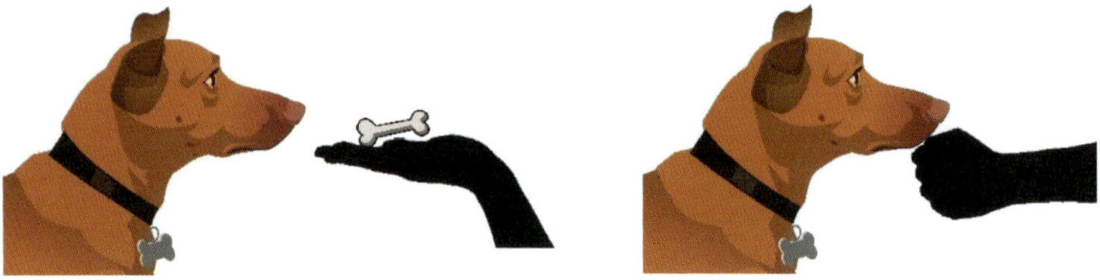

Step 4- Repeat this process until the dog can keep his nose out of your hand for 3 seconds. Once you can leave your hand open without them diving in, pick up a treat with your other hand and take it to their mouth.

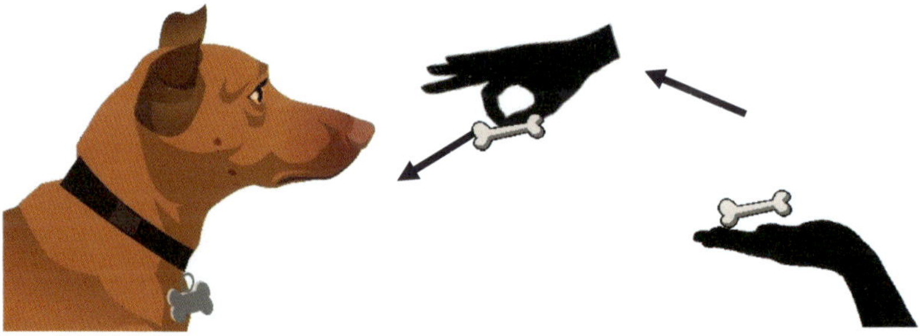

Step 5- If they keep their nose away from your hand, feed them more. Any time they try to dive their nose in, shut it again.

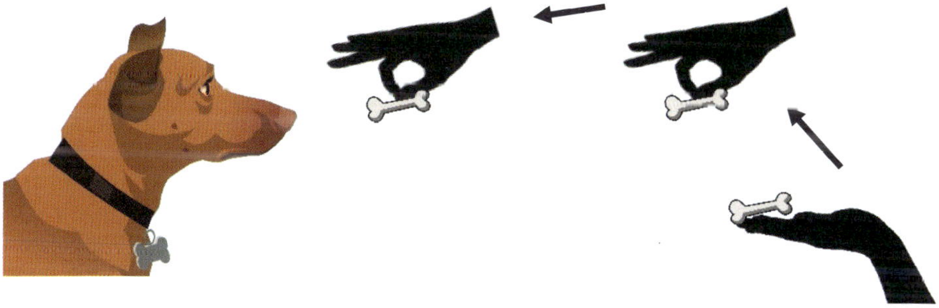

Step 6- Next, wait for eye contact or looking way from the treat before you praise and reward them with the treat.

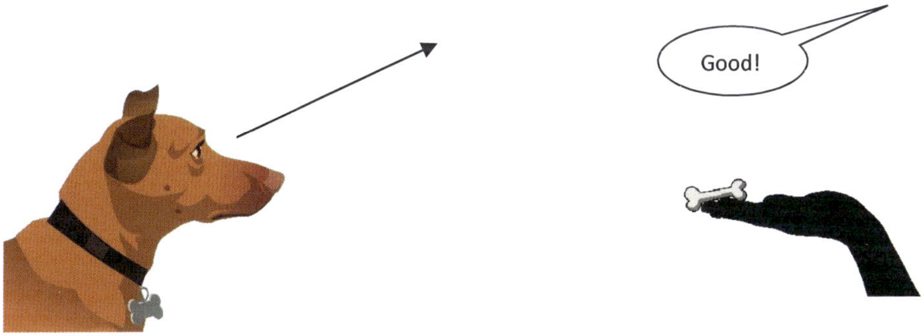

Step 7- Repeat the whole process with the food on the floor instead of in your hand. Cover the food with your hand when they dive into get it.

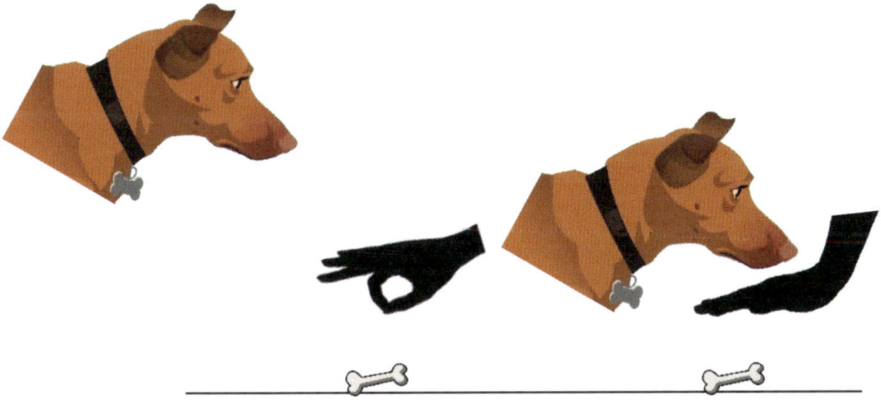

The Attention Game

Many people do not realise how important it is that your dog checks in with you and gives you attention, until you lose it. If your dog keeps an eye on you and comes to you for direction, it means you do not have to keep an eye on them! The more you reward a behaviour, the more likely it is that the behaviour will increase.

Step By Step Guide

Step 1- Ensure your treat bag is full of pea-sized treats and have your dog off-lead in an enclosed area.

Step 2- When your dog looks at you, immediately praise this behaviour and throw a treat away from you. This resets the dog for another round. Repeat.

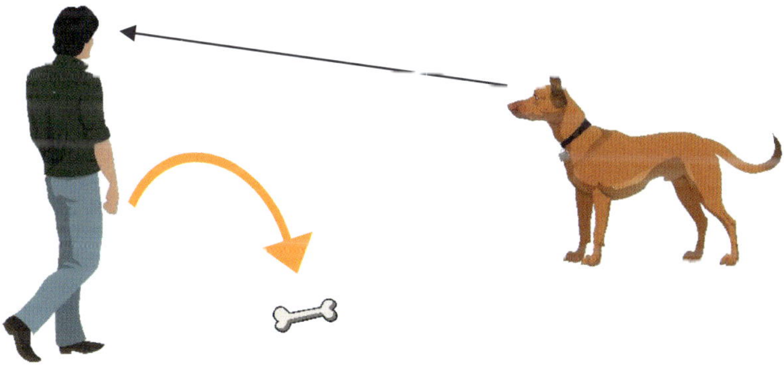

Step 3- As your dog starts to understand the game they will become less distracted by their surroundings and get quicker at looking at you.

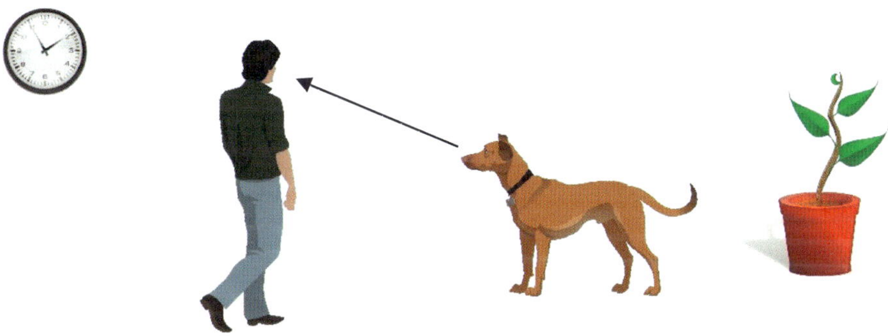

Step 4- Practice this is many different environments, increasing the distractions slowly.

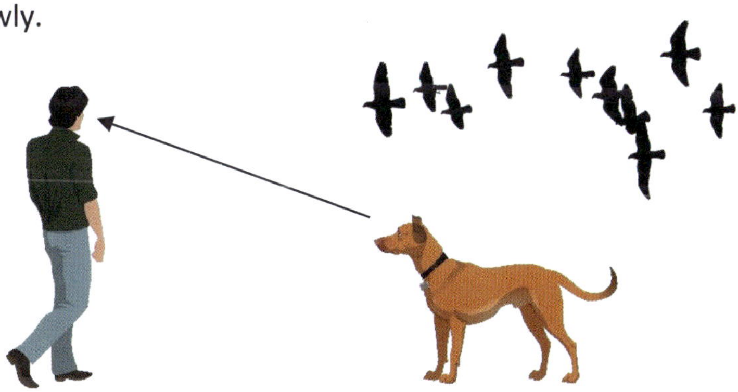

Step 5- Even if you're not playing the game and your dog checks in with you, reward it! This will be a huge bonus once they are off-lead out on a walk.

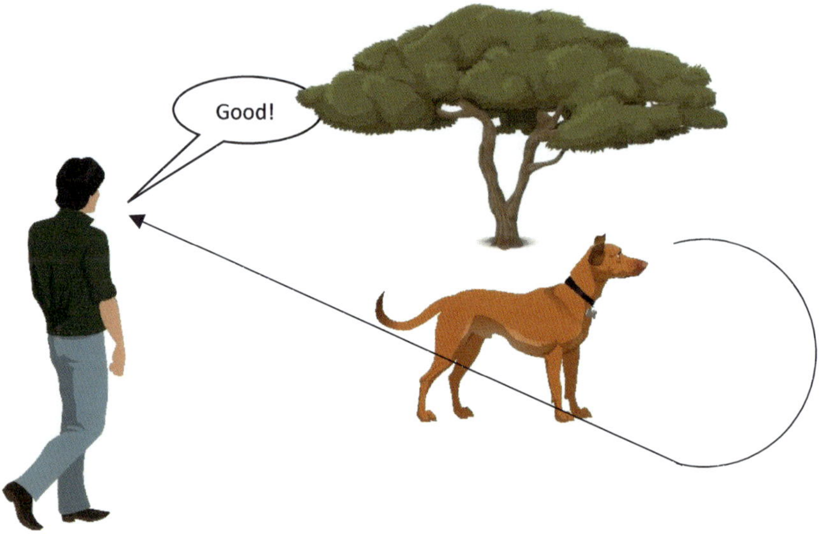

Top tip: Ensure the reward you are using can compete with the environment and the distractions you are in!

Toilet Training

Whether you have a new puppy or an older dog, appropriate toilet training is a major part of house life. Even if they have been previously toilet trained they may need a refresher in a new home. We need to remember when we toilet train dogs never to scold them if they have an accident, this will just make them nervous to ever go to the toilet in our presence.

Step By Step Guide

Step 1- When you first take the dog home take them straight outside to where you would like them to toilet. If they do toilet in the correct place, reward them with at least 5 treats to make it memorable.

Step 2- Give them as many opportunities as possible to get it right and take them outside often (2 hrs adults) (1 hr puppies), especially after waking up, eating or playing.

Step 3- If they have an accident do not scold them. Pop them outside and clean the area with a biological cleaner which breaks down the smell of ammonia.

Step 4- Once they know where to go to the toilet, some dogs will make you aware when they need to go (Barking, pacing or scratching the door). Look out for these signs and reward them if appropriate.

Step 5- Once they are going to the toilet in the right place, you can add a cue. This will help when you are out and about and need them to relieve themselves. To do this, ask them if they want to go "outside" and say "get busy" before they relieve themselves. They will then associate the word with this behaviour as they are being rewarded with a high volume of treats.

Top tip: If your dog stands by the door or procrastinates, go outside with them on lead.

Hand Targeting

Being able to get your dog to touch and follow your hand on cue, is a great way of moving them around without physically manipulating them. This can be especially useful for getting them onto a set of scales at the vets or getting them off the bed or sofa.

Step By Step Guide

Step 1- Present your hand to the dog. They are naturally curious creatures, so may approach your hand to sniff or lick it. Mark this behaviour with a clicker (see page 69) or a word like "Good" and reward them.

Step 2- Put your hand behind you back before you present it again; this resets the situation ready to repeat the behaviour. After a few repetitions, up the criteria so that the dog gets more reliably closer to touching your hand.

Step 3- Once the dog is happily touching your hand, move it around. Down low, high up, to the left, to the right and encourage them to follow it by making it into an exciting game. Practice manoeuvring them around and onto objects.

Top tip: If you have a very visual dog you can use this as part of their recall cue, they will come racing back just to bump your hand.

Stay

Ensuring your dog will stay on cue can be an extremely important skill, which may be utilised in dire situations. Remember each dog will learn at a different pace and we need to give them more opportunities to get it right, than to get it wrong. The difference between stay and wait: stay means, stay where you are until I come back to you; wait means, wait until I tell you to do something else. Therefore, it is extremely important never to recall the dog out of a stay.

Step By Step Guide

Step 1- Ask your dog to either sit or down; start with the position they are most likely to stay in. Count to 3 in your head, praise and reward (they must stay in the position you placed them in). If they get up at any point, lure them back to where you placed them and start again but make it easier.

Step 2- Once step 1 is repeatedly successful, place them in position and instead of counting to 3, wiggle your feet (not too enthusiastically!). Praise and reward.

Step 3- Now we can step out with one foot, whilst keeping the other in place. Praise and reward. Then start stepping away and return. Praise and reward.

Step 4- Think of the 3 D's; distance, duration and distraction. Remember to only increase one aspect at a time. For example: If you want a long stay don't move far way.

Top Tip: Put your stay to the test! Can they stay if you:

- Run away
- Do a star jump
- Go out of sight
- Lay on the floor
- Turn your back

Leave

What do we want "Leave" to mean to our dog? When I teach leave, I want the dog to know not to bother trying to get the object as they are never going to have it and I have something even better for them. Therefore, using our self-control exercise as a foundation works well, but cannot be used to teach an effective "Leave" as all the dog is doing is waiting.

Step By Step Guide

Step 1- Place an uninteresting object which your dog is never going to have on the floor e.g. a brick. Pop your dog on lead, ensuring you are far enough away that they can move close to the object without reaching it.

Step 2- As soon as they turn away from the object and look at you, praise and reward. Move around the object, repeating this exercise until your dog is happily turning away from the object and looking at you.

Step 3- Now that your dog knows the game. Ask them to "Leave" just before they turn to look at you. If you think you will struggle saying the word "Leave" positively; you can try "Boring" instead.

Step 4- Loose lead walk (see page 56) past the object. When the dog looks at the object say "Leave", praise and reward when they come with you.

Step 5- Repeat step 4 with multiple different objects e.g. cone, orange, packet of pasta, cereal box.

If the dog ever reaches the object, use your most exciting voice, a handful of treats or a toy waved in their face and bring them away. Always reward them for coming with you.

Greeting People Appropriately

A dog's ability to greet people nicely has become a very important skill, especially because of the recent changes in dog law. Instead of reprimanding jumping, we need to ask the dog to do something incompatible with jumping. In this case the dog cannot be jumping up if it is sitting or lying down.

Step By Step Guide

Step 1- As soon as you are made aware of people either coming to the door or in the distance out on a walk, pop your dog on the lead. However, it is worthwhile inviting a group of friends to visit to practice repetition at home and in the street.

Step 2- Either step on the lead or anchor it to your tummy to prevent yourself pulling on It. Ensure your dog has enough room to stand comfortably but not jump up.

Step 3- Ask any approaching people to only greet your dog once he is sitting. If at any point he gets up, they must back away again until he is sitting again.

Step 4- They may calmly greet the dog, encouraging the dog to keep their feet on the floor by dropping treats. Nose on the floor = feet on the floor.

Step 5- It is also good idea to teach the dog to sit whilst somebody comes into your house. If they get up whilst the person is entering, the visitor leaves again.

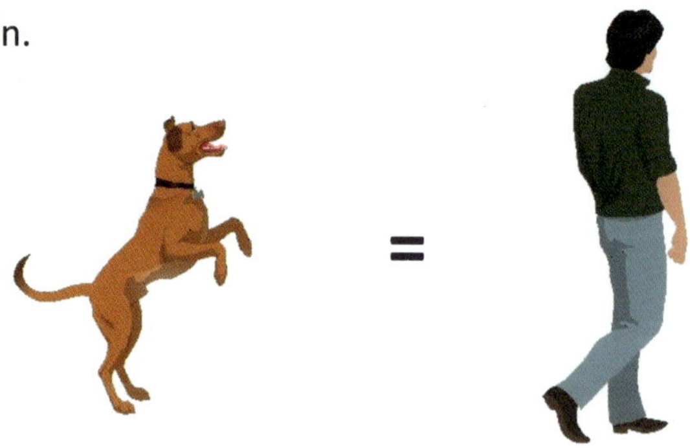

Step 6- Once your dog reliably keeps their feet on the floor and the lead stays loose, you can take the lead off. If you dog likes to hold clothes, only allow them to greet a guest when they have a toy in their mouth.

Top Tip: Remember to generalize greeting people to lots of different environments and situations. Just because your dog knows how to do it at the park, it does not mean they know how to do it at home.

Play Manners

It is a really important skill that your dog has manners when it comes to playing. This is because when they become over excited we need to ensure that they can still control their weaponry, to prevent any accidental injuries.

Step By Step Guide

Step 1- Before we start, we need to ask them for a behaviour such as sitting calmly, before we invite them to play with our cue word.

Step 2- Whilst playing, if at any point teeth hurt your skin, stop the game and walk out of the room shutting the door behind you. Games are not fun if the dog has to play them on their own.

Step 3- If you want the game to stop or pause so you can begin again, there are 3 options you can use to teach the dog to release a toy, these depend on your dogs' individual personality.

A- Some will be happy to exchange their toy for a treat.

B- If you make the toy boring, by holding it still or dropping it, the dog may let go.

C- Keep exchanging toys until the dog predicts that you will give them the other one once they have dropped the first. At this point you can ask for a polite sit before you start playing again.

Step 4- Once the dog is used to letting go of the toy in order to continue the game we can put it on cue. Just as the dog is about to let go of the toy use your cue word "give" or "thank you".

Step 5- Play Jazz up and settle down. Really amp the dog up, making the game super exciting, then ask them to settle. This very good practice for controlling energy and quickening recovery from excitement.

Top Tip: If they get hold of something they cannot have, you can use this cue to get it back. Remember not to chase them, as it may turn into a game!

Flirt Pole

Teaching your dog self-control can be difficult as it something the dogs has to exercise to achieve, just like working a muscle. We can do this by making it a fun game and letting them learn themselves what gets the results. Flirt poles are useful for this as you can use them to mimic the movement of prey. You can make you own with a rod, elastic and an exciting toy.

Step By Step Guide

Step 1- Ask your dog to either sit or down. Count to 3 in your head, praise and reward them with play. If they get up at any point, lure them back to where you placed them and start again but make it easier.

Step 2- Once step 1 is repeatedly successful, place them in position and instead of counting to 3, wiggle the toy (not too enthusiastically!). Praise and play.

Step 3- Now we can present the flirt pole, place the dog in position and wiggle the pole (not too enthusiastically!). If they stay put, praise and play with the pole.

Step 4- Now you can begin to get them to drop the toy and do some other behaviours before being rewarded with the toy again. If they change position when you are moving the toy, flick it up into the air out of their reach, they will soon learn they only get the toy when they follow the 'rules' of the game.

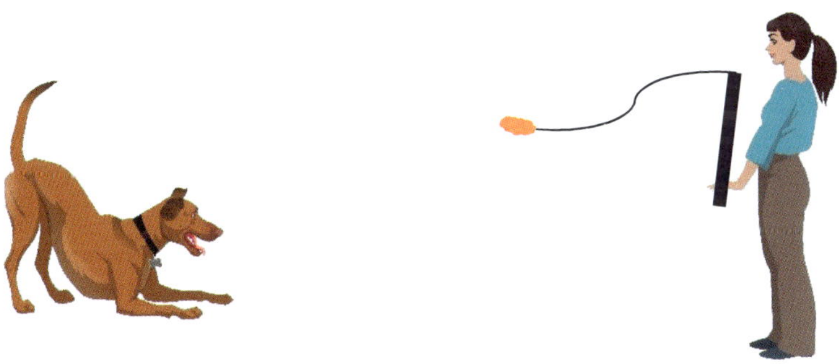

Handling and Grooming

It is important for a dog to tolerate or better yet, enjoy being handled and restrained, as this is a part of everyday dog care. Therefore, it is important that we help teach the dogs that this is an enjoyable process and not one that they need to be worried about. The main difference between a hug and a restraint is the dog's perception of the handler.

Step By Step Guide:

Collar Touches

Step 1- Lure the dog in front of you using a treat so you have easy access to their neck. Put your hand lightly on their collar and mark this success with the word "Good!" remove your hand immediately and reward them.

Step 2- Repeat step 1, touching the collar for longer periods of time. If at any point the dog moves away, let them, we do not want to make them feel as if they are trapped.

Step 3- Once the dog is happy having his collar touched, start holding the collar instead, building up the time slowly.

Step 4- If you feel the dog is ready for this you can start to bring in collar grabs. Reacting calmly when someone grabs their collar in an emergency, could save their life. Slowly increase the speed of the grabs ensuring you jackpot each one!

Handling

Step 1- Begin by stroking the dog somewhere they feel comfortable i.e. their back. Whilst your hand is still in contact with them, mark this with the word "good" and reward them.

Step 2- Slowly begin to run your hand from their back to down their legs, praise and reward. If they pull away, let them, just go back a step until they feel comfortable again.

Step 3- Work your way up to being able to touch all over their body. If there are sensitive areas, work on these particularly slowly with lots of rewards. Commonly sensitive areas: paws, ears, tail, rump, muzzle, collar.

With an unfamiliar dog, assume all of these areas are sensitive and work up gradually to touching them. Work between the areas that the dog finds comfortable and also less comfortable, this will help to build positive associations quicker.

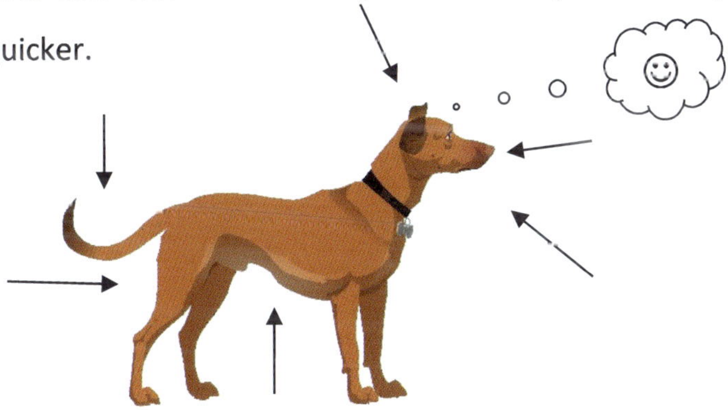

Top Tips:

- Try not to rush as this can excite the dog or make them more nervous.
- Allow the dog to move away if they feel unsure.
- Talk the dog through the process; your voice can be really comforting and you can even teach them the names of their body parts.

Grooming

A dog should be comfortable and confident with you touching them before you attempt to groom them. All dogs need to be groomed on a regular basis; this removes dead hair and is a good time to do a routine health check for any lumps or skin irritations.

Step 1- First we need to desensitise the dog to the equipment you will be using. Hold the piece of equipment and when the dog sniffs it, mark this behaviour with the word “good”. If the dog appears worried, make it easier and mark them for simply looking at it.

Step 2- Stroke the dog's back with your hand, immediately followed by a stroke with the brush (so the dog barely notices) praise and reward.

Step 3- Slowly progress to longer strokes and brushing in different areas. Always allow the dog to move away if they are unsure and take the process back a step.

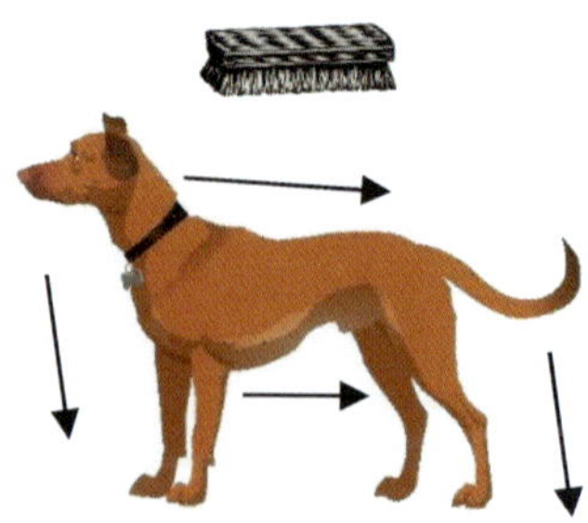

Step 4- Extend the amount of time and grooming which is done before you praise and reward the dog. If there is a particularly awkward or difficult matt in the dog's fur, do not attempt to get it all done in 1 session.

Step 5- Work between areas which the dog find pleasant and those which it finds uncomfortable. This will help build a positive association quicker. Ensure you are always tailoring the experience to the needs of the individual.

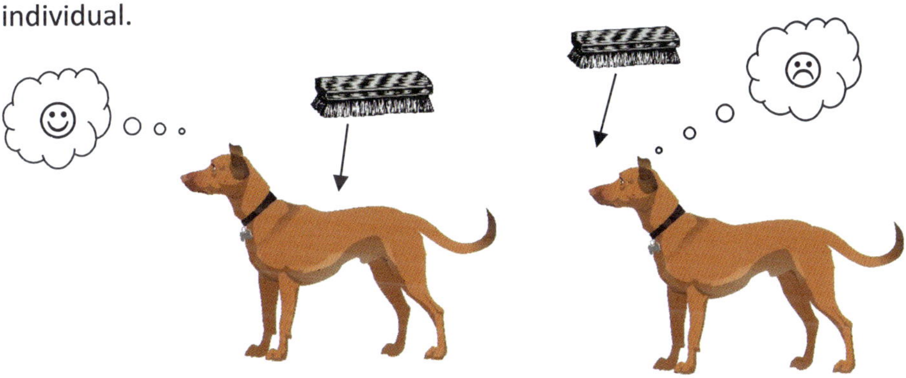

Step 6- Once the dog is confident with being brushed all over with one piece of equipment; you can begin the process again with a different grooming tool. If a dog will need to be clipped, they can also be desensitised to the sound of the clippers.

Top tip: Give the dog something to do, a KONG to lick or a hoof to chew. This will keep them less fidgety and busy.

Loose lead Walking

Teaching your dog not to pull you along is important for safety and also makes walking your dog more enjoyable. When the lead is loose, the dog gets to move forward and gets rewarded. If the lead goes taut they get nowhere.

The more consistent you are, the quicker the dog will learn and once this behaviour has turned into a habit, food rewards can be used less and less.

Step By Step Guide

Step 1- Get your dog's attention and lure them to your side with a treat. Praise and reward them in place. As soon as possible stop holding food in your hand and praise and reward from your pouch or pocket.

Step 2- Walk forward two paces, if the dog stays with you reward them with a treat.

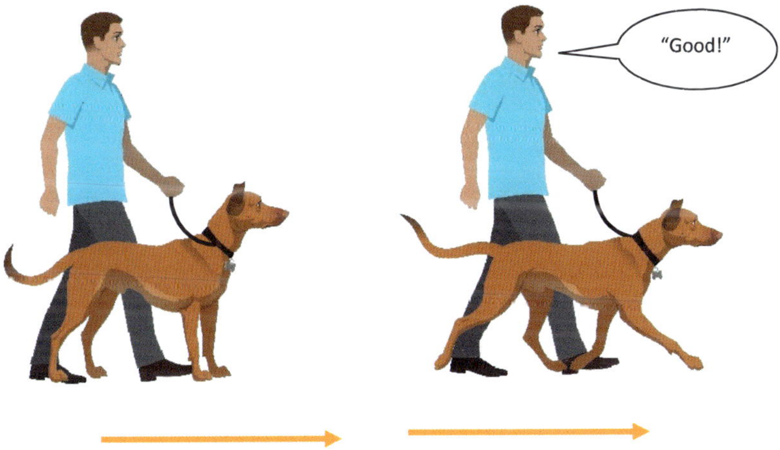

Step 3- If at any point the dog pulls out, STOP. Encourage them to return to your side before you set off again.

Top Tip: Practice in a low distraction environment such as your garden or the same strip of street, and slowly build in the distractions.

Step 4- Gradually increase the number of paces you walk before rewarding. Ensure you vary the number of paces, so you are not always making it more difficult.

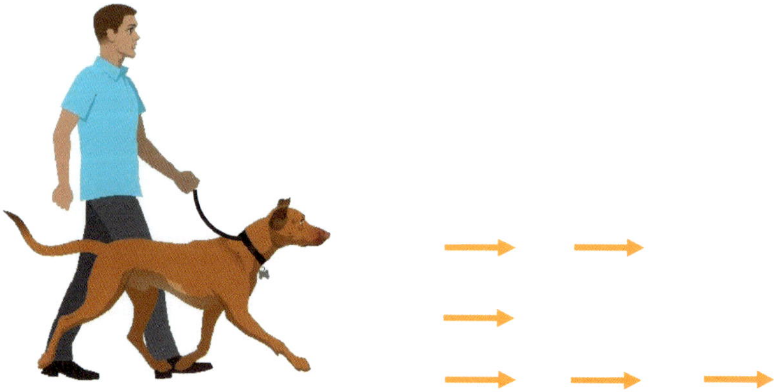

Top Tip: It is best to use a harness whilst the dog is learning, so they do not damage their throat from pulling.

Step 5- Reward your dog when they check in with you, as we want to encourage this important behaviour.

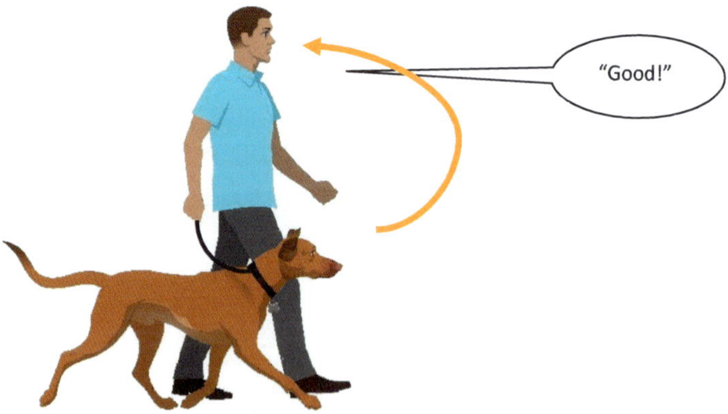

Top tip: Remember, how you handle your lead impacts your dog. If you see something worrying in the distance, try not to tense the lead, as the dog will pick up on your subtle cues of anxiety.

Recall

Teaching your dog to come back on cue is one of the most important things they need to be taught in order to be safe off-lead. If you always want your dog to come back when you call, you need to continue to reward above average recall responses, especially when they could be having more fun elsewhere.

Step By Step Guide

Step 1- Decide what your recall cue will be: "come", "here" or a whistle. Whistles can be easier for some dogs as it is a consistent sound which they can easily tune into.

Step 2- Start inside your house with your dog in the same room. Use your cue and drop a handful of high value food on the floor by your feet for the dog to eat.

Step 3- Continue step 2 until you're confident your dog will respond if you were to use your cue in a different room. Now we need to start lightly

holding their collar before we give them the treat to ensure they do not learn to grab it and dart off.

Step 4- Continue step 3 until you're confident your dog will respond from any room in the house. Then you can move the training into your garden, where there may be slight distractions.

Step 5- We need to fit and acclimatise your dog to wearing a harness. The reasoning behind this is so we can attach a long line to the harness to keep control of the dog in public if needed. Reward your dog for putting his head in and out of the harness and eventually wearing it.

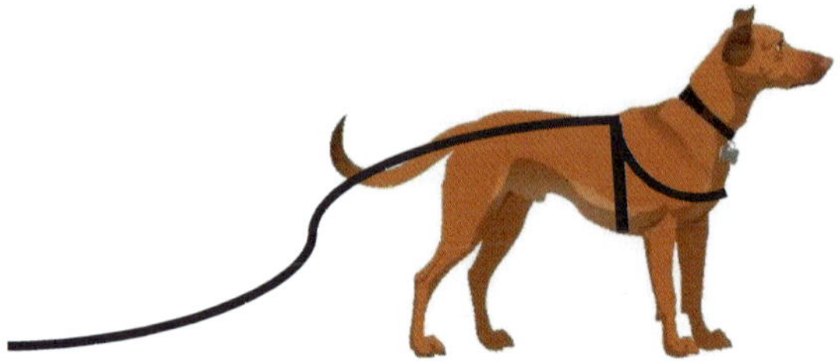

Step 6- Time to go out and about! In the beginning ensure you keep hold of the end of the line. Randomly cue your dog to recall so they do not associate the cue with their fun ending. If the dog does not respond, reel them in and ask for another behaviour before setting them off again.

Whenever the dog approaches the end of the line let them know by telling them "steady", they will begin to understand that this is their maximum distance. If they decide to check in with you of their own accord, reward them! We want to encourage this.

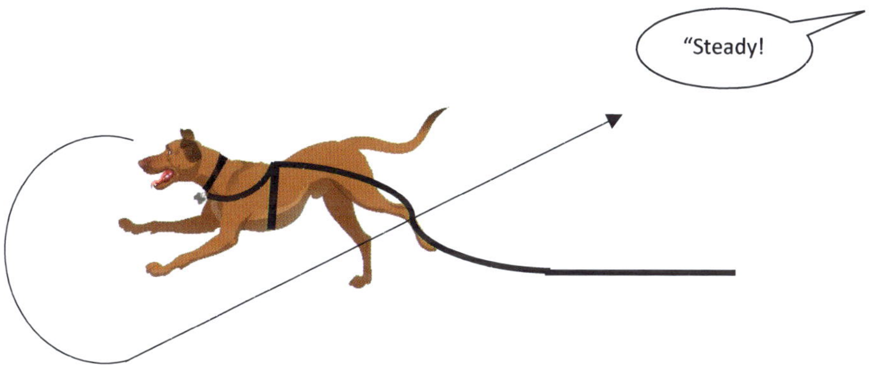

Step 7- A good game to play with your dog is recalling between 2 people. Let the line trail, but be ready to step on the end if needed.

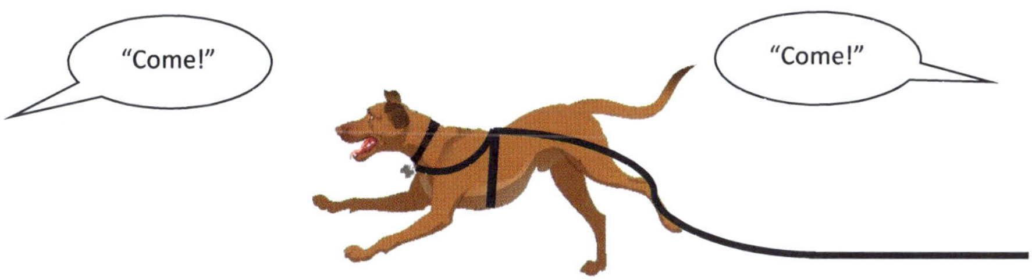

Step 8- After a number of weeks, in many different environments and with an array of distractions, if you feel your dog is ready and recalling with enthusiasm 95% of the time, we can unclip the line.

If at any point your dog starts to be unresponsive to your cue, clip them back onto the line. You do not want them to practise this behaviour and have your dog deemed 'out of control'.

Top Tip:

1. No reward for below average responses. I.e. Dawdling
2. Small reward for above average responses. I.e. Plodding back
3. Good reward for good responses. I.e. Running back
4. Jackpot award for amazing responses. I.e. Sprinting back

The better the response the better the reward!

Dog - Dog Interactions

When picking the dog you wish to interact with your own, ensure they complement each other and are not both easily over aroused. Pick a dog which you know is fine with other dogs whilst you socialise your new dog. Remember to only move onto the next step once both dogs are comfortable.

Step By Step Guide

Step 1- Start all dog-to-dog interactions with some parallel walking. Pick a distance at which the dogs are comfortable at and walk parallel to each other (see page 103). Gradually decrease the distance. If at any point the dogs react or get over aroused increase the distance again.

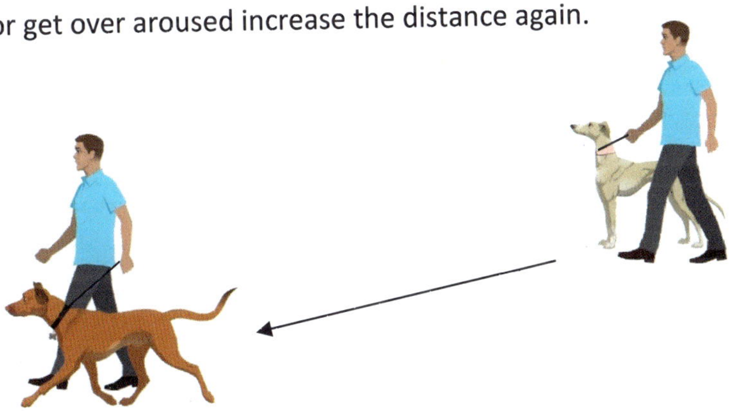

Step 2- Keeping at a comfortable distance, do some basic training with the dogs. If they are unable to concentrate on their handlers, you are too close. Increase the distance and do some more parallel walking before trying again.

Step 3- Reward the dogs for calmly looking at one another when walking. If one dog goes in for a butt sniff whilst the other is busy sniffing, let them. Remembered to keep all interactions to a couple of seconds each initially.

Step 4- Ensure the dogs never meet face to face on lead. This is an unnatural greeting and can escalate very quickly. Allow the dogs to arc (see page 101) around each other to sniff if they must meet on lead and keep the meeting very short.

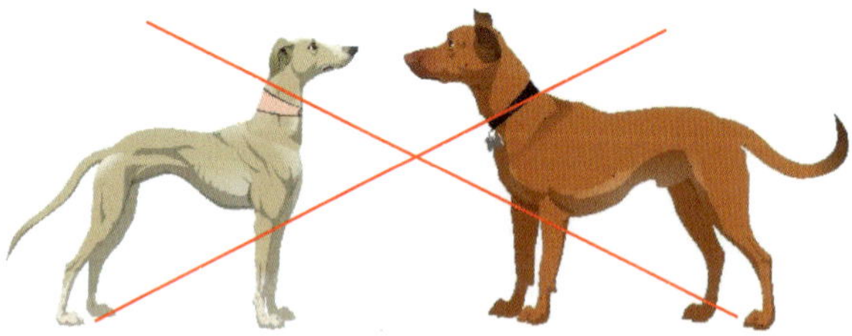

Step 5- In a safe, enclosed area let the most nervous dog off first, in order to gauge their reaction to the other dog. If you think the on-lead dog would get overexcited with the off lead dog, keep them on a lead or long line, at least until the other dog initiates play.

Positive interactions include:

- Give and take "you chase me then I'll chase you". If you think one dog is doing more chasing then the other hold the chaser's harness lightly and sees how the other dog responds. If they come back for more, they are perfectly happy to continue playing.
- Play bows and loose, wiggly bodies.
- Ignoring one another, sniffing or wanting to work with you.

Look for:

- Tension and stillness in the dogs' bodies signalling uncertainty or warning.
- Mouth tightly closed signalling tension.
- Lots of short breaks. You may have to put short breaks in yourself if the dogs are unable to do so.
- The dogs displaying calming signals to one another, and the other dog responding appropriately.

If they do not respond appropriately to one another, you may have to step in.

Calming signals

These are behaviours displayed by a dog during conflict or stress, attempting to calm the situation which is worrying them. They are mostly used towards other dogs to communicate their intent but also used towards people in an attempt to communicate. If they are ignored the dog may stop using them and escalate from stress to aggression in order to protect themselves (see the ladder of aggression on page 96).

Top Tip: Remember these signals are context-specific, so if you see a dog displaying these signals, look at the rest of the situation too.

- Nose/Lip Lick
- Yawning
- Turning head or body away
- Paw lift

- Soft blinking eyes
- Play bow
- Sniffing the ground
- Walking slowly
- Shake off

Behaviour

Modification

Hand Feeding

Hand feeding can be so beneficial for you and your dog to create an initial understanding and bond. Not only are you creating a positive association between following your hand cues, you are creating a more attentive and focused dog. Using the dog's dinner not only cuts down on treats, but allows your dog to be mentally stimulated and work for their food.

Use the technique of luring to get the dog to follow your hand into various positions. You can very quickly teach them new tricks, manners and impulse control, especially if you praise and reward what you like.

Top Tip: Hand feeding helps create a positive association with people being around a dog's food!

The Basics of Clicker Training

Clicker training is a method of teaching which uses a marker to tell the dog that the behaviour they have performed is good or correct and they will be rewarded for it. The marker doesn't have to be a clicker, it can be a whistle or a word. However; a clicker is a consistent sound that dogs are easily able to tune into, which makes it perfect for training.

Step By Step Guide

Step 1- Click the clicker and give the dog a treat, pause and repeat. The dog will begin to anticipate a treat after the click. 1 Click = 1 treat. If you stop treating when you use the 'click', the 'click' will become meaningless.

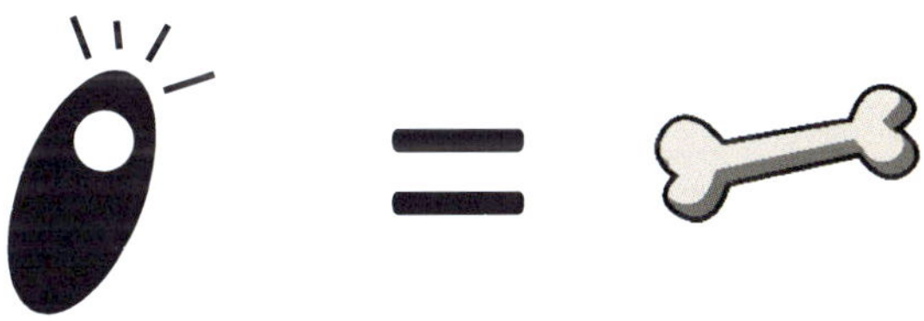

Step 2- Repeat step 1 until the dog anticipates a treat at the sound of the click. You will be able to tell when this occurs as your dog will hear the click and look for the treat.

Top Tip: Use small, smelly and easily palatable treats for the best association and frequency.

Step 3- Now we can start using the 'click' as an indicator that they have performed the correct behaviour. For example, you ask for a sit, as soon as their bottom hits the floor you 'click' and give them a treat.

Step 4- You can use the 'click' for any behaviour you want to see more of, because the more something is rewarded the more likely the behaviour is to occur. In addition 'clicking' for the absence of a behaviour will lower the frequency of the behaviour occuring. For example, when your dog stops barking 'click' and reward.

Shaping

Shaping is a training strategy used to move towards a specific behavioural goal, without the use of luring. We do this by adhering to criteria, which enables us to work in steps to reach the final behaviour. Each criterion is successfully reached, praised and rewarded before moving onto the next. Ensure you take it at the dog's pace and build their confidence if they are struggling, before moving on.

Example with elevated platforms: Useful for teaching self-awareness of the body and giving a fixed station to work upon.

Step By Step Guide:

Step 1- Praise and reward any interaction with the platform (stepping towards, sniffing, and looking).

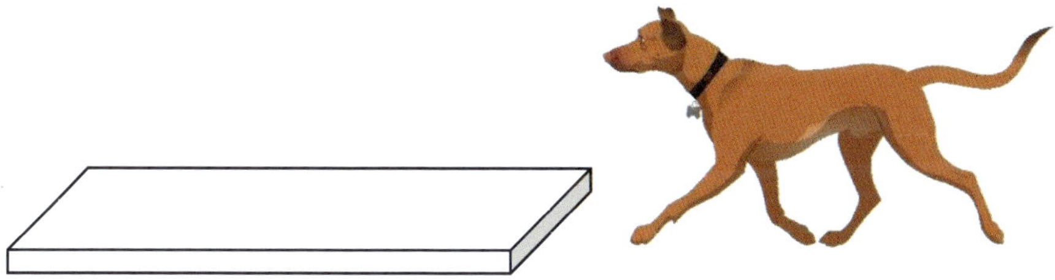

Step 2- Reward one foot on the platform. Throw the reward away from the platform to reset.

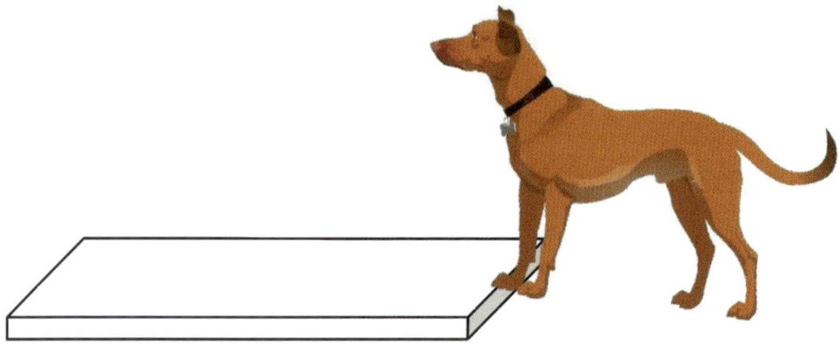

Step 3- Reward movement on the platform i.e. more feet.

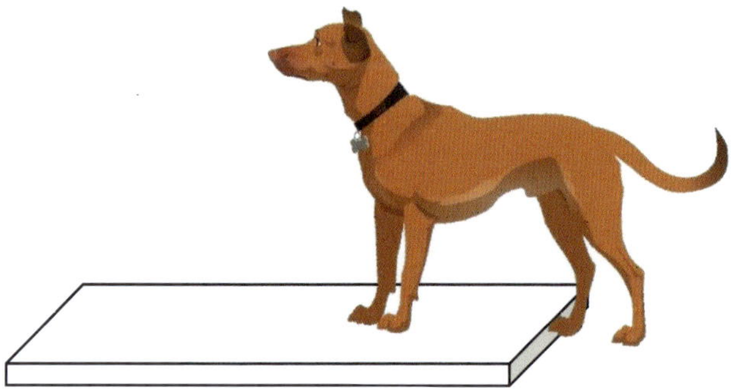

Step 4- Once all 4 feet are on the platform, reward in the standing postion. Do not reward sitting or laying on the platform as we don't want this to become a default.

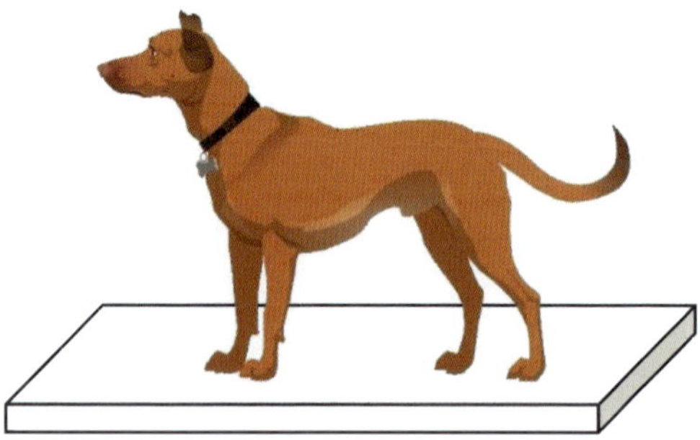

Top Tip: Look at the area you want the dog to move to.

Shaping a Retrieve

Retrieves can be used in sport, as a trick or a way to exercise your dog. Some dogs will naturally enjoy retrieving and do it automatically, whilst others need to be taught. A successful retrieve requires the handler to send the dog to recover a specific object and bring it back to the handler. You can only begin retrieve training if your dog is happy giving up toys to you willingly when asked.

Step By Step Guide

Step 1- Pick a toy or any object you wish to teach the dog to retrieve. Make the toy exciting by wiggling it round and being very interested in the toy.

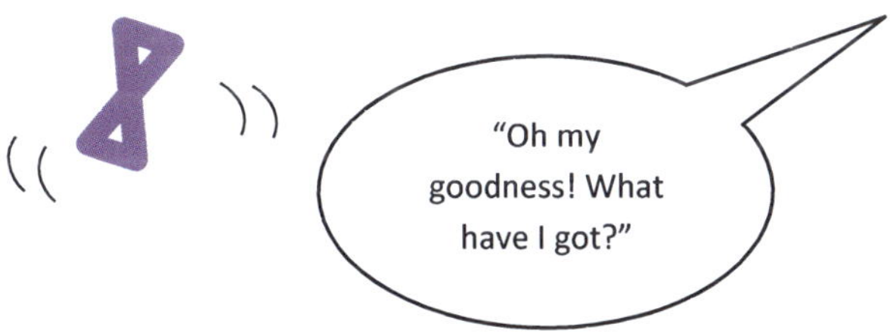

Step 2- Allow the dog to approach the toy and hold it in their mouth (you also need to hold it). As soon as they do this, mark the behaviour "good" and reward with a treat.

Top tip: If the dog does not want to put they toy in their mouth try to make the toy more exciting, try a different toy or reward the dog for sniffing the toy and build up to holding it.

Step 3- Repeat the dog holding the toy in its mouth multiple times, until the dog is eager to hold it. Now we need to build duration. Instead of praising the behaviour as soon as the dog holds it, count to 3 in your head before you praise and reward.

Step 4- Once the dog is able to hold the toy in his mouth happily for 3 seconds, you can let go of the toy once he is holding it. Count to 3, put your hand back on the toy, praise and reward.

Hand off 1,2,3 Hand on

Mark & Reward

Step 5- Without holding the toy, put it on the floor and encourage the dog to hold it in their mouth, praise and reward.

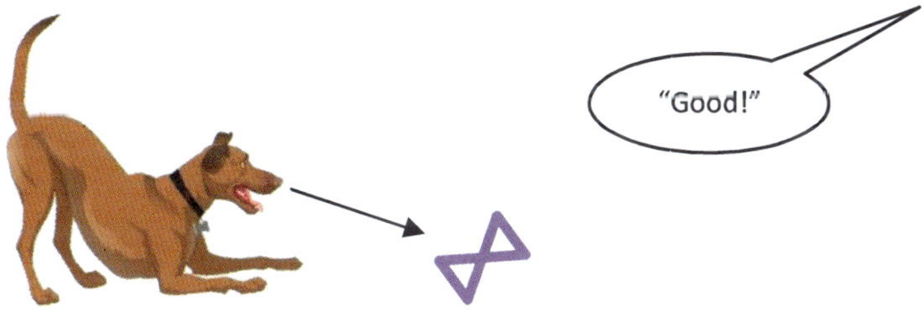

Step 6- Once the dog can hold the toy and pick it up, praise and reward.

Step 7- Once the dog can hold the toy and pick it up, encourage them to put it in your hand. Praise and reward.

Top tip: If the dog is finding any step difficult, make it easier for the dog by taking it back a stage and only moving forward once they understand.

Step 8- Time to increase distance. Start to place the toy further away from you, encouraging the dog to pick it up and bring it to your hand.

Step 9- Throw the toy and encourage the dog to retrieve it! Jackpot this success!

Top tip: Once the dog finds this game fun it should become self-rewarding, so you no longer need to reward with food.

Remember you MAY need to reteach this process with other objects.

The Premack Principle

An individual dog's preferred or goal behaviour, will reinforce a less preferred behaviour. Therefore, what the dog wants becomes dependant on performing the behaviour you want, we can call this a life reward and regularly use this in training.

Examples

Example 1- Sitting makes the door open.

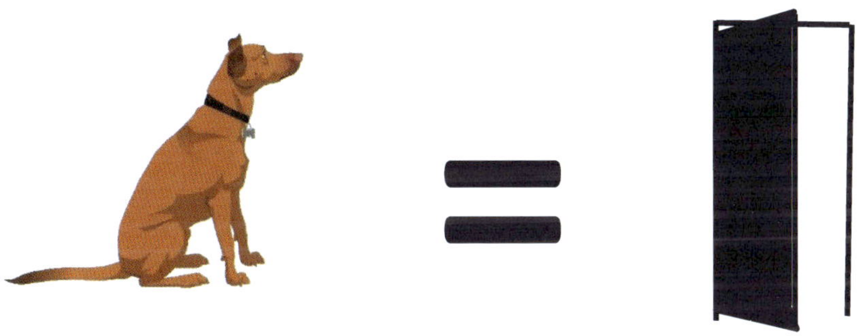

Example 2- walking on a loose lead = sniffing privileges

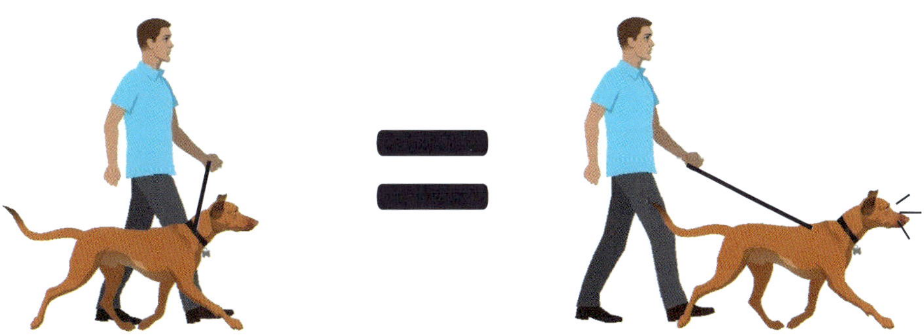

Example 3- Coming back when called = playing in the river

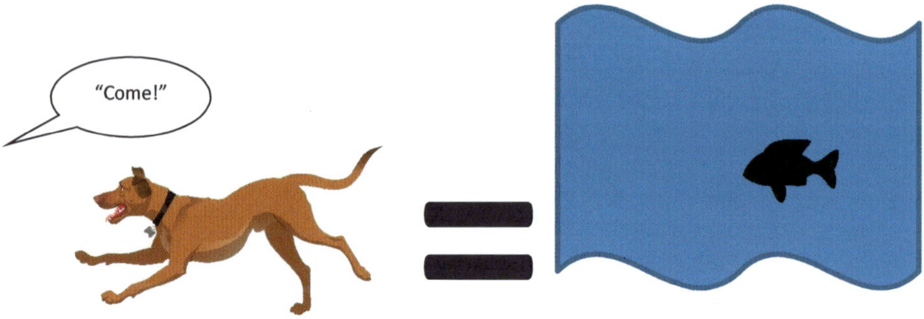

Example 4- No barking = access to look out the window

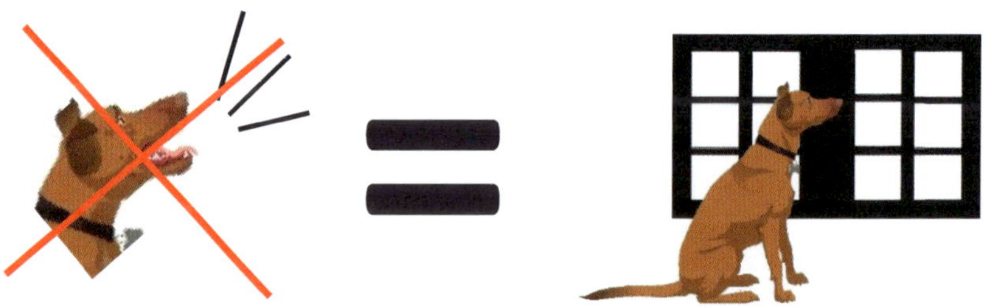

Example 5- Giving up the ball = chasing the ball

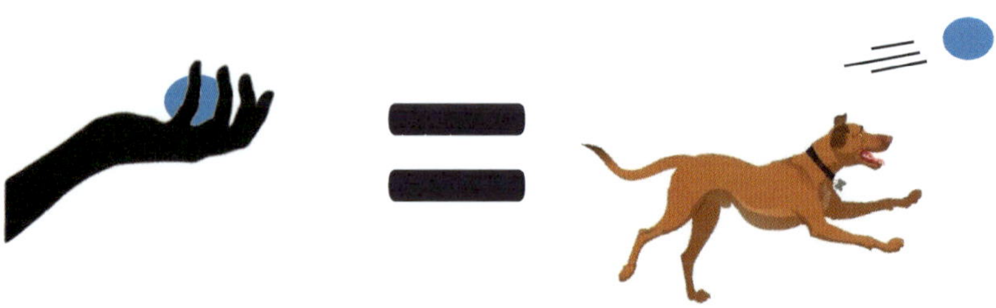

Redirection

"No" is a word we use very often but it does not mean much to our dogs. When we use "no" we generally want the dog to stop what they are doing, but we are not telling the dog what an appropriate alternative would be in order to achieve the same result. This leaves the dog to guess and make mistakes. Redirection is the use of one word that solves the 'problem' behaviour.

Step By Step Guide

Step 1- Evaluate the situation in which you would like behaviour to change. What behaviour can you ask for that is not compatible with the unwanted behaviour? For example, sitting instead of jumping around when visitors come round.

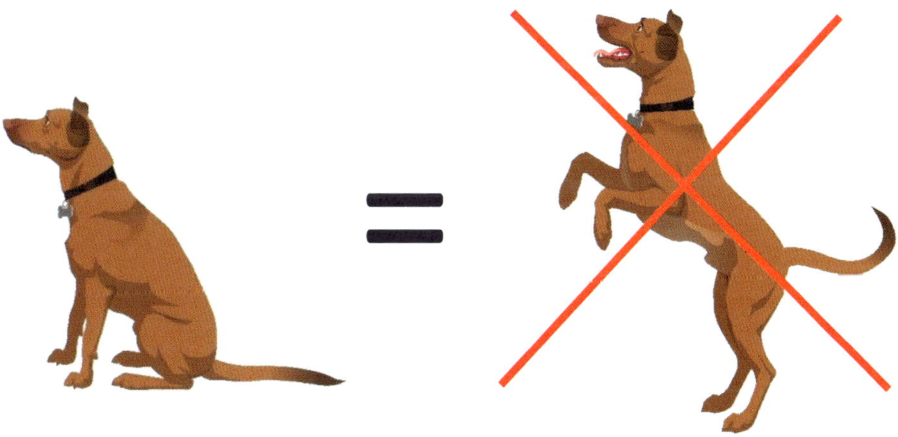

Step 2- If the dog does not know the behaviour you would like to swap the unwanted behaviour for, we need to teach it.

Step 3- Now we need to set up the situation so we can practice replacing the unwanted behaviour with the new behaviour. If your dog is over aroused, it may take a lot of practice and reinforcement before they use this alternative behaviour as their default.

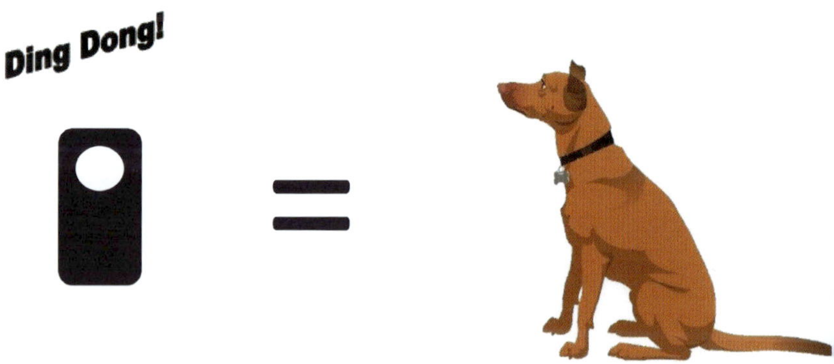

Chewing

Dogs chew things for many different reasons: they may be teething, bored, stressed or frustrated. Chewing and licking can help relieve stress and frustration as the action releases pleasurable endorphins. We need to help teach our dogs what is acceptable to chew on and give them activities to keep them mentally stimulated.

Step By Step Guide

Step 1- Put away any items that the dog can reach which are of value to you.

Step 2- If they are chewing on something inappropriate, either lead them away from the item and/or give them something they are allowed to chew on.

Step 3- Ensure you have plenty of things for them to chew on: squidgy toys, deer antlers, dried feet/ears, wet and frozen rag toys.

Step 4- Keep them mentally stimulated and give them their dinner in a KONG or puzzle toy. Alternatively you can do some fun trick training and use their dinner as rewards.

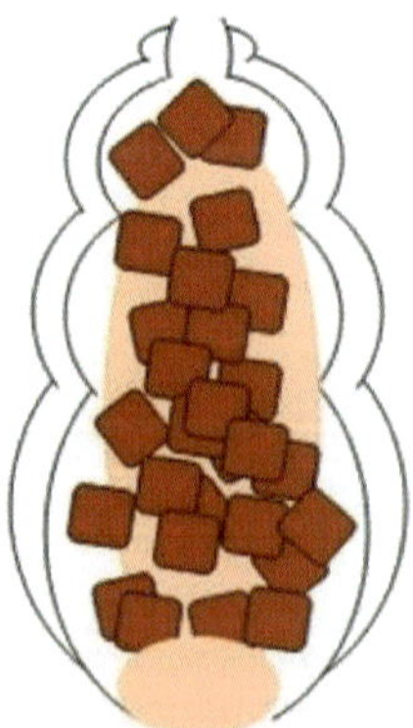

Top Tip: Rotate their toys every few days to prevent them from becoming bored of them.

Mouthing

Dogs and puppies mouth for a variety of reasons. It is a completely natural and normal behaviour for a puppy and they need to practice it to learn bite inhibition. However, we do need to teach them self-control to prevent them inflicting pain, there are three ways in which we can communicate this.

Step By Step Guide

Scenario 1- When teeth hurt skin, yelp "Ouch!" Some dogs will understand that this means they hurt you and they will stop. We don't want to scare them but allow them to realise that it hurt! However, some dogs may become exited and think this as an invitation to play, so it may be a case of trial and error.

Scenario 2- If teeth hurt skin, promptly leave the room and shut the door behind you for 10 seconds. Lack of weaponry control means no attention. Repeat as necessary.

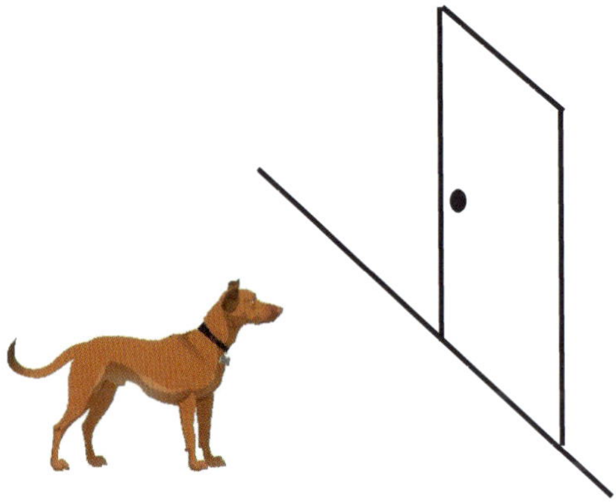

Scenario 3- When teeth hurt skin, redirect the dog onto something they are allowed to grip onto i.e. soft toy. Ensure you ask them for an alternative behaviour before you give them the toy; this is to ensure you are not rewarding the mouthing. This may be the best option for puppies who may be in pain due to teething. We can also provide them with a frozen rag toy to help soothe their gums.

Ensure that if the dog is mouthing when excited, you try to keep all play calm. Engage their brain and do some training together.

Separation Anxiety

The key to preventing separation anxiety is teaching your dog to be comfortable on their own. However, it is still possible to teach your dog to be happy on their own even if they have already developed anxiety. The most important thing is to slowly build up the amount of time that they are left, ensuring they are comfortable at each stage before moving on.

First teach the dog that being alone when you are home is enjoyable. When you do begin to leave them, very slowly build up the amount of time that they are alone for.

Tips to help your dog cope:

- Ensure your dog is exercised before you leave so they are more likely to take a nap.

- Turn the radio on and give them a KONG, chewing is a comforting and stress relieving behaviour so the radio becomes a cue to relax when paired with a KONG.

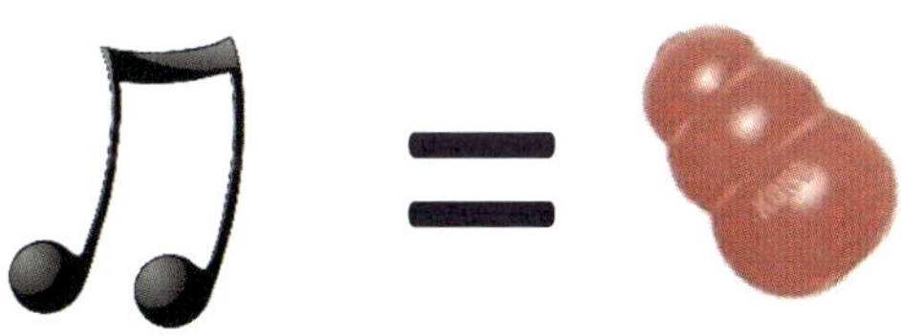

- Give your dog a safe place such as a crate. Follow the crate training guidelines.

- Leave them with an item of clothing with your scent on it.

- Set up a video to record what your dog does when you are out, this will help you to determine whether they are distressed or not.

- Make friends with your neighbours and ask them to let you know if your dog is distressed.

- Try using pet remedy which is a herbal remedy or Adaptil, a calming pheromone. Another option is something called a thunder shirt, which gives your dog the same comforting feeling, similar to when a baby is swaddled.

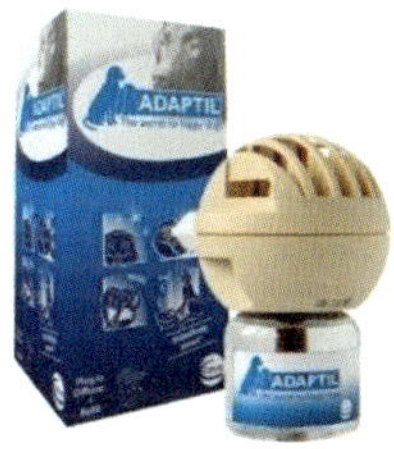

If your dog has been destructive or made a mess, do not punish them. They have exhibited this behaviour because they are anxious. If you punish them they may become more anxious.

Resource Guarding

Be a giver, not a taker

Resource guarding is when a dog becomes defensive over a valued object and may growl or snap to prevent the removal of the object. Many owners unknowingly teach their dog to guard by interfering with their food or resources (ironically to try and prevent it!) this backs up their theory that you will take their things away when they feel unsure.

If your dog is growling at you this may make you upset, but it is important to not punish your dog for it, as it is a communicative signal that the dog does not feel comfortable. If you start to punish these behaviours, you would most likely create a dog that will bite without warning. It is important to give them space and not make them defensive.

Step By Step Guide

Step 1- Manage the environment to prevent possible harm e.g. if you have children use baby gates to separate the dogs and the children when eating.

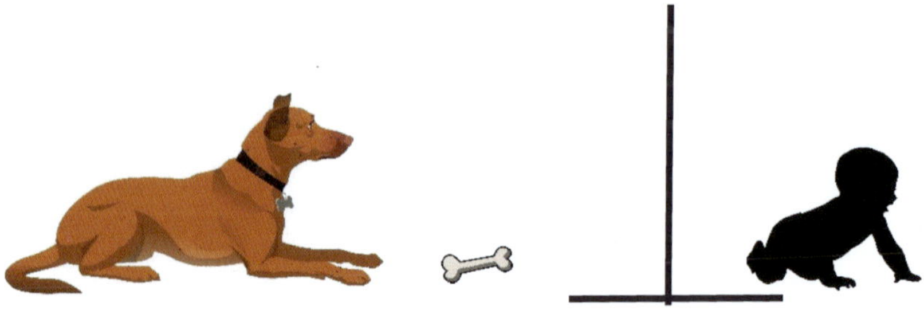

Step 2- Create a positive association between you approaching their resources. Ensure that you always add something tasty to their bowl when you approach rather than taking something away. If they currently guard their food bowl just throw the tasty morsel to them until they let you approach happily. If they guard their bed, throw them treats every time you walk past, so that someone coming close is a good thing!

Step 3-If they guard the sofa, teach them the on and off game. Encourage them up and then throw a treat off and say "off". Do this until they will happily get on and off. This means they will be happier with you approaching as you will not be forcibly removing them from the sofa and being on the floor is more rewarding than being on the sofa.

Step 4- If they steal or guard things that they have found or should not have, always sound happy, "what a clever dog, what did you find!?" This will encourage them to come and show you what it is. Then, if what they have is dangerous or important you can swap it for a treat or toy. Do not chase them, as you could make them defensive or teach them that stealing equals a fun game of chase.

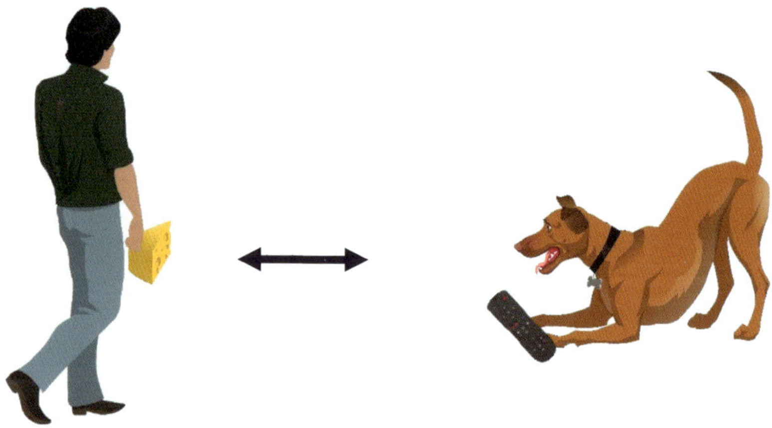

Top Tip: Remember all behaviour is a symptom of an emotional state.

Reactivity

The Reactive Dog

Handling and Training

Reactivity is a common problem and can be caused by many different things. At Suppawt we define reactivity as: ***an increase in 'inappropriate' coping behaviours, caused by the appearance of something which creates fear, frustration, excitement or anxiety in the dog.*** It is important to be considerate and understanding to help your dog overcome this problem. The reasons for the behaviours elicited through reactivity are:

- SAFETY- distance increasing behaviour.
- INFORMATION- how will the stimulus respond?
- FUN- generally a breed specific behaviour which is reinforcing to carry out.
- RESOURCE PROTECTION- anything which the dog values and is anxious may be taken.

Step By Step Guide

Handling

Top Tip: If at any point the dog's behaviour has escalated to the point where they cannot think rationally (reached their reactivity threshold) i.e. lunging, barking or unable to listen to you, create more distance between yourselves and the stimulus.

Scenario 1- Getting your dog safely away from a stimulus which causes a negative reaction. Run one of your hands down the lead as near to the dog as possible; this is your anchor point. Holding the anchor point still, pivot around in front of your dog and take them off in the other direction. Reward them for coming with you.

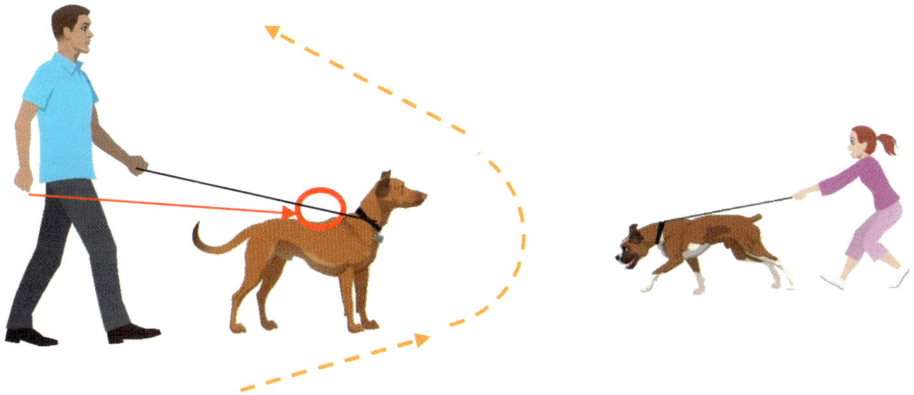

Scenario 2- Dogs naturally arc around other dogs or stimuli they are unsure of, so giving them the space to do this helps them cope with a situation in which they may otherwise react.

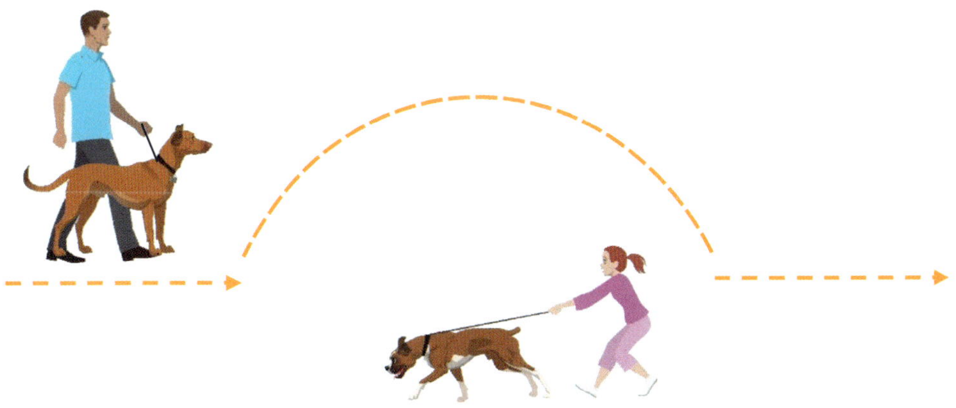

Step 1- Changing the dog's emotional response to the stimulus is the first step in changing their behaviour. In this step, every time the dog sees the negative stimulus feed them a high value reward regardless of their behaviour.

Top Tip: Don't worry! You are not rewarding the behaviour at this point. This is because the dog is responding emotionally to the stimulus and you cannot reinforce an emotion.

Step 2- The dog then begins to anticipate that every time they see the stimulus, something good happens. The negative stimulus becomes a positive.

Step 3- Now that your dog's emotional response toward the stimulus has improved, you can wait for an appropriate behaviour in the presence of the stimulus before you reward them. i.e. being calm, looking away, looking at you.

Step 4- Decreasing the distance between your dog and the stimulus should only be done when the dog is comfortable at the starting distance. Look for relaxed posture and being attentive towards you. The moment they start to stiffen or become alert, this is the distance you should work at **before** the dog gets over their threshold. Reward them highly for looking and then refocusing on you.

Look out for:

Relaxed Dog

- Wiggly body
- Open/soft mouth
- Relaxed posture
- Tail is at half mast

Alert Dog

Close to reaching threshold

- Tense body
- Closed/tight mouth
- Tail high and still

Top Tip: Remember, if you become tense and anxious at the sight of a trigger, you can make your own dog reactive! Keep the lead loose but take up the slack, breathe and work through it.

Ladder of 'Aggression'

The Ladder of Aggression was first developed by Dr Kendal Shepherd, in which she depicted the escalation of behaviour to the perceived stress or threat of a stimulus. In a perfect world, the dog would start at the bottom of the ladder and if its displays of avoidance are ignored, the dog would make its way up the ladder step by step.

However, some dogs may learn that certain signals are ignored and may begin to miss rungs of the ladder and escalate more quickly. Furthermore, the dog's level of arousal when it jumps onto the ladder, will depend on where the dog starts and how quickly it escalates.

A point to note is that not only can a dog move up the ladder, but it can also move back down the ladder to calm itself as the threat decreases.

Top Tip: The more you watch dogs interacting, the easier you will find it to see these subtle signals. Once you notice these, you will know if you need to step in and intervene or when to reward your dog for making good choices.

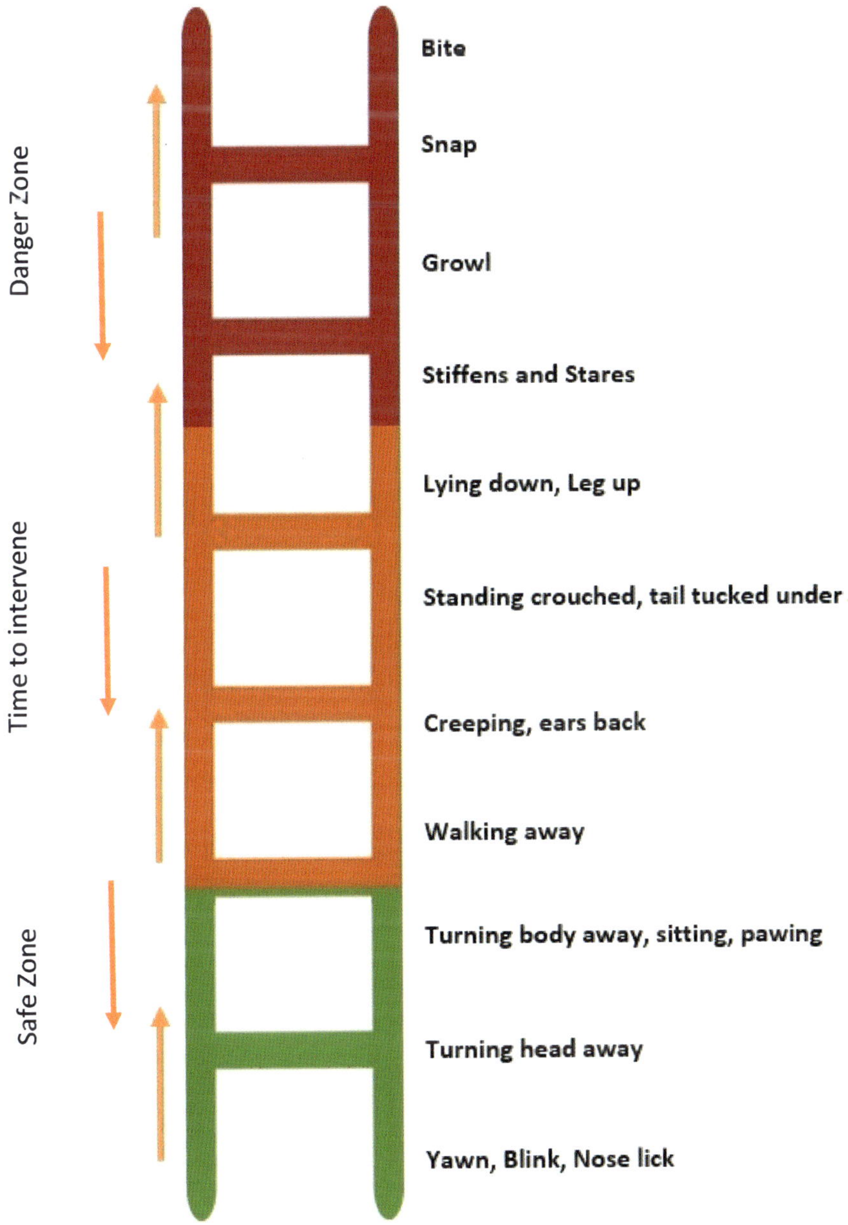
Danger Zone
Time to intervene
Safe Zone
Bite
Snap
Growl
Stiffens and Stares
Lying down, Leg up
Standing crouched, tail tucked under
Creeping, ears back
Walking away
Turning body away, sitting, pawing
Turning head away
Yawn, Blink, Nose lick

Trigger Stacking

Stressors which the dog may not usually react to, when occurring in short succession, can trigger a dog to go over threshold. Their reactivity threshold is the dog's capability to cope with stressors before reacting to them. For example, a dog-reactive dog may be fine with another dog 100 feet away, but once they reach 20 feet away this is too much for the dog and means the dog goes over threshold barking and lunging at the other dog.

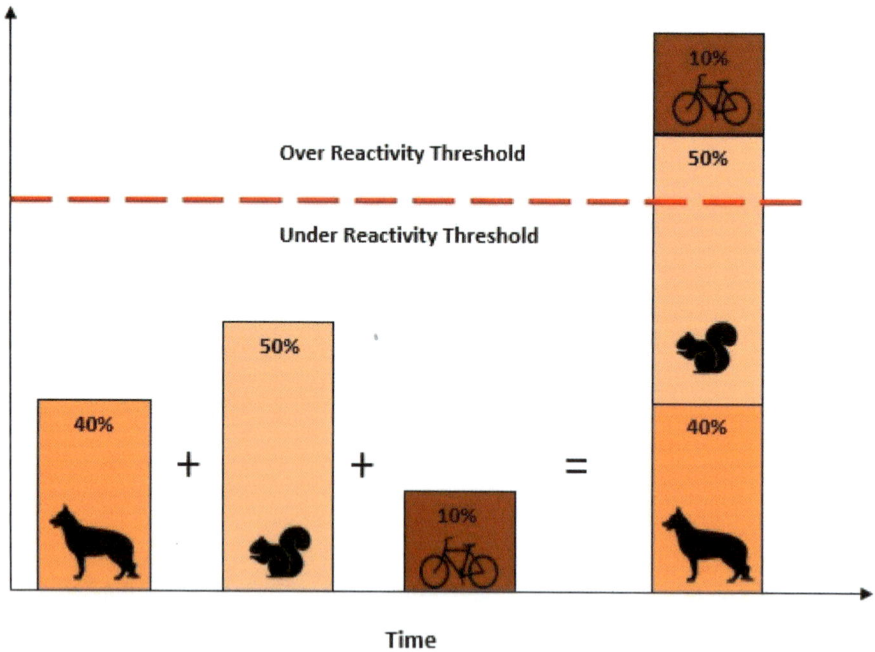

Classical Conditioning

Classical conditioning is the process of pairing something that causes one response, to a stimulus with a different response. The 1st stimulus then becomes a predictor of the 2nd stimulus. Therefore, the 1st stimulus causes the behaviour response of the 2nd stimulus.

This can be helpful to you in situations when your dog responses to a something in an 'inappropriate' way i.e. barking. We can then alter the way the dog responds to that stimulus by changing their emotional response at a distance in which the dog is able to learn.

Step By Step Guide

Step 1- Your dog barks and lunges every time it sees a cat [Example]. Whatever the dog's reaction we feed him a high value treat (i.e. cheese) whilst standing and watching the cat.

Top Tip: Don't worry! You are not rewarding the behaviour at this point. This is because the dog is responding emotionally to the stimulus and you cannot reinforce an emotion.

Step 2- Your dog begins to anticipate that when a cat appears he gets cheese. So instead of barking at the cat he begins to look at you expecting his cheese.

Step 3- You reward the attention your dog is giving you and are now able to manage the situation in a controlled manner by rewarding more appropriate behaviours, like sitting and looking at you. You now have a quiet and controlled dog even when he sees a cat.

Arcing

Arcing is a useful strategy to use for avoiding a stimulus which may cause an unwanted reaction. It uses the dog's natural instincts of avoidance, using curving to give themselves space.

Step By Step Guide

Step 1- You see something in the distance which you would like to avoid. Focus your dog's attention on you and get them to walk by your side.

Step 2- As you begin to approach the stimulus, swing your leg closest to the dog out to the side and move off, curving away from the stimulus before eventually re-joining your path. Reward your dog for coming with you.

Step 3- Practising the leg swing and putting it on cue makes it much easier for future use. To do this use your cue word “this way” or “turn” just before you swing your leg out to move off. Your dog will soon begin to associate the word with changing direction and a reward.

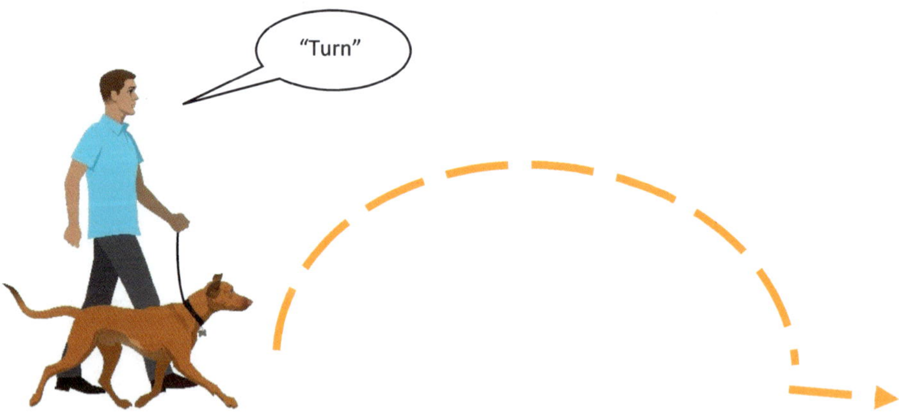

Top Tip: Avoid only practising this when a stimulus you want to avoid appears, you may accidently turn this into the cue for ‘something’s coming’.

Parallel walking

Parallel walking is a useful strategy to have in your tool box, especially when it comes to introducing new dogs to each other or training a reactive dog. The idea behind parallel walking is to keep the dogs at a distance from each other in which they are under threshold (not reacting). Over time we decrease the distance between the dogs until they are able to walk next to each other comfortably.

Step By Step Guide

Step 1- Keep your dog at your side, furthest from the other dog. If they are reactive to other dogs, reward every time they look in the other dog's direction.

Step 2- Start at a distance in which both dogs are showing calm body language and are under threshold. Both sets of dogs and people set off in the same direction.

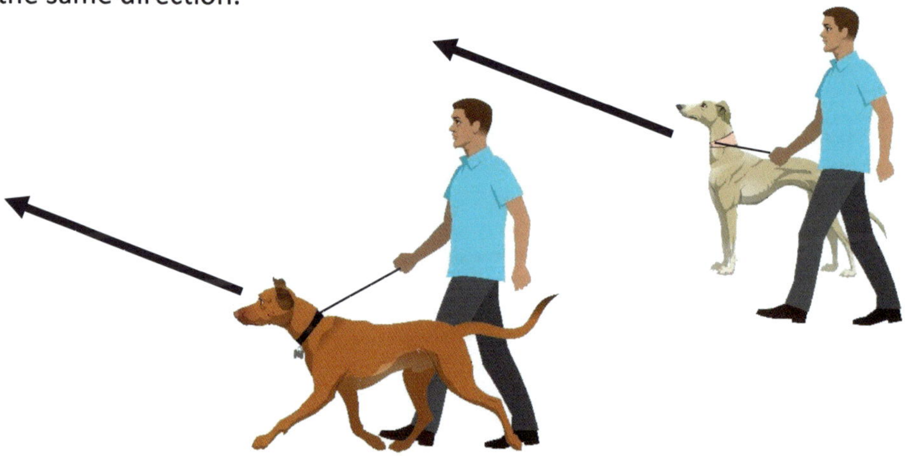

Step 3- Slowly reduce the distance by stepping towards each other one step at a time. If at any point one of the dogs become uncomfortable, create more distance.

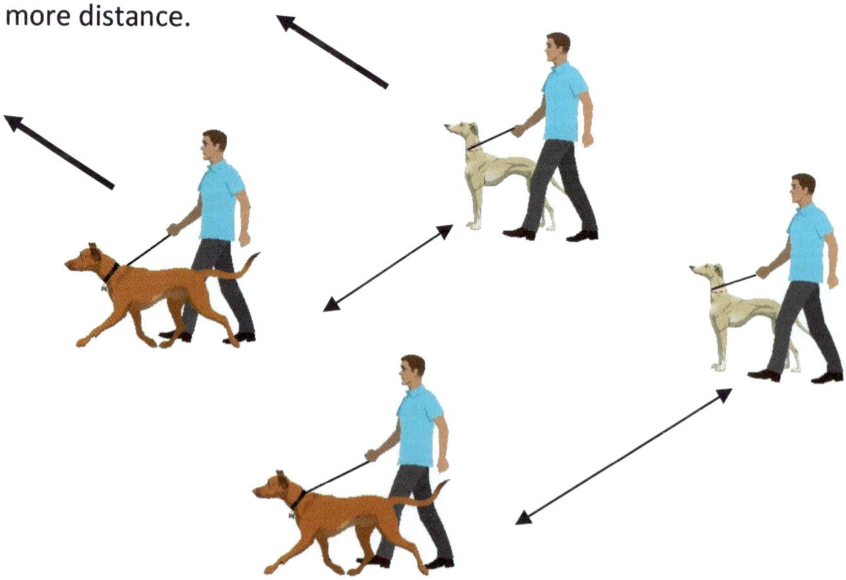

Splitting Up

Splitting up is a great way of avoiding a fight with another dog. If you end up nose to nose on lead, tension can build very quickly and behaviour may escalate. You can also use it when you need to get your dog under control if they are pulling at the end of the lead.

Step By Step Guide

Step 1- When your dog is pulling at the end of the lead. Anchor your hand and the lead to your stomach.

Step 2- Run your free hand down the lead just above the dogs back and grip firmly. This creates a point to pivot around.

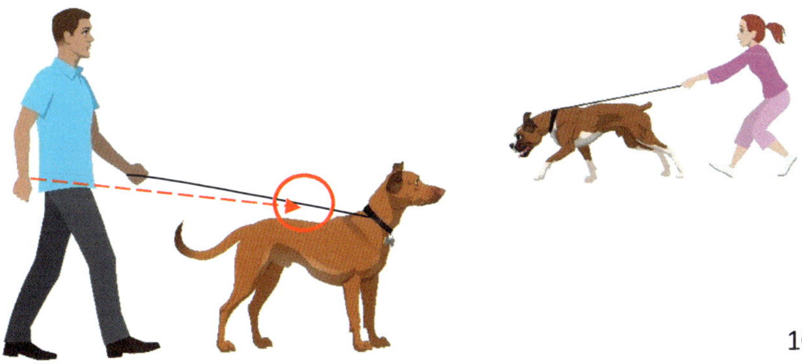

Step 3- Keeping your hands in position, move around in front of your dog, crossing their path and take them off in the other direction. Reward your dog for coming with you!

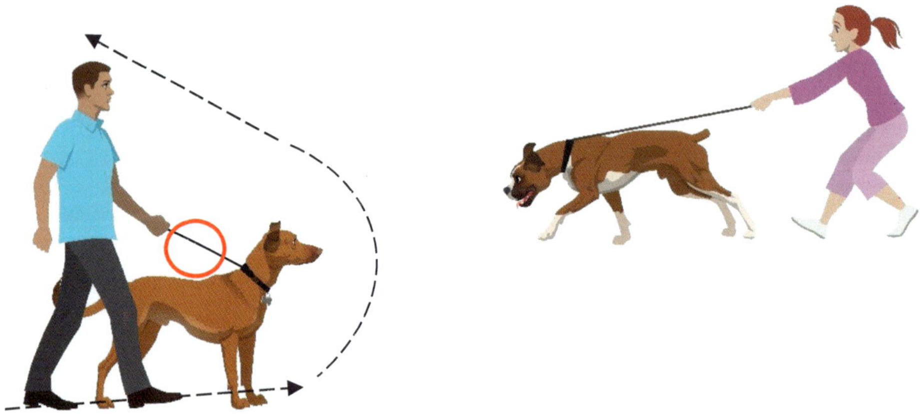

Step 4- Practising this manoeuvre and putting it on cue makes it much easier for future use. To do this use your cue word "this way" or "come along" just before you step round to move off. Your dog will begin to associate the word with this movement and changing direction.

Anxiety Reduction

Just as with humans, dogs can also suffer from anxiety and stress disorders. Even if they don't normal suffer with anxiety, there can be events in their life that dogs can find particularly stressful. Stress and anxiety reduces the speed of learning and can reduce the effectiveness of the immune system. Therefore, it is important to help reduce stress and anxiety as much as possible.

Easy access- products on the market:

Adaptil – A pheromone that is released by a bitch to comfort her puppies and help them feel secure.

Pet Remedy- works with the pet's own natural calming mechanisms by mimicking GABA, a natural calming agent present in all mammals.

Thundershirt- A pressure wrap used to reduce anxiety and promote relaxation.

Other products on the market:

- NutraCalm
- Zylkene
- Clomicalm
- Through the dogs ear- sound CD

Diet:

What we feed our dogs can have a profound effect on their mood. Increasing the levels of serotonin in the brain assists in learning alternate or new behaviours, combating behaviour problems.

Some specific diets have been formulated to up the dog's intake of serotonin, or alternatively you can manipulate your own dog's diet. (Strong, V., 2009. COAPE. Applied Canine Nutrition; The implications of diet on behaviour.)

Veterinary intervention:

A knowledgeable vet can supply you with helpful medications to reduce your dog's anxiety whilst you work on their training. Ensure that you ask the vet for the pros and cons of each medication and how long it takes to become effective, before making an informed choice.

Top Tip: Ensure your dog has a portable safe place that they have associated with relaxation and positive events. This could be a mat, bed or crate.

Please note these may be effective for some dogs but not for others, as all dogs are individuals.

Storms and Fireworks

It is very common for dogs to be sensitive to sounds such as fireworks or thunder. It is important to make these experiences as pleasant as possible in order to create positive associations with these events.

Tips to help your dog cope:

- Keep the dog indoors during fireworks or storms.
- Shut the curtains and windows and turn the TV or radio up louder.
- Do not fuel you dogs fear by worrying over them as this will make them feel there is something to be worried about.
- You can provide comfort if the dog seeks it, with reassuring strokes, calm voice and body language as you cannot reinforce fear. Try not to react to the fireworks yourself.
- Distract them with a really tasty stuffed KONG or a food puzzle.
- Make a safe haven for your dog where they can hide and feel safe and secure.
- Do not punish any behaviour you deem inappropriate which is linked with fear (toileting in the house).

Remember all dogs have different coping strategies

Future Preparation:

Buy a socialisation sound CD or play clips on YouTube at a barely audible level to begin with.

1. Associate these sounds with fun training, treats, games and puzzles.

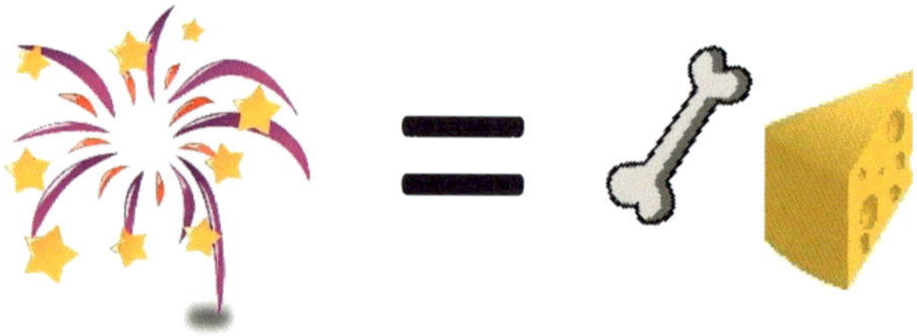

2. Over many weeks slowly raise the level of these noises, if your dog reacts to them you have gone too fast and need to reduce the volume again.

3. When you think your dog is ready, do this at night time for the usual fireworks or storm effect.

You can also try some products which are known to help certain dogs. Pet Remedy, Adaptil, Thundershirt or speaking to your vet about sedatives.

Muzzle Training

Muzzle training is **not** solely for the use of aggressive dogs, it is also useful for those with a high prey drive, those that eat things they shouldn't, those that are fearful in particular situations and those in pain. A Baskerville muzzle has an open grid, allowing the dogs to breathe freely, pant to cool themselves down and receive treats.

Step By Step Guide

Step 1- Hold the muzzle in your hand and praise and reward the dog for approaching and sniffing it. This will encourage the dog to continue this action in order to get reinforced.

Step 2- Up the criteria by only praising and rewarding the dog for touching their nose to the muzzle.

Step 3- Once they are comfortable with step 2, swiftly move on to only reinforcing for putting their nose inside the muzzle.

Step 4- Once they are enthusiastically participating with their nose in the muzzle, withhold the praise for 3 seconds in order to increase the duration that they keep their nose in the muzzle.

Step 5- Once the dog is happy with step 4, hold the muzzle straps at the back of the head. Feed the dog a treat through the holes of the muzzle and then remove the muzzle. Repeat.

Step 6- Clip the muzzle on at the back of the head. Feed the dog a treat through the holes of the muzzle and then remove the muzzle. Repeat.

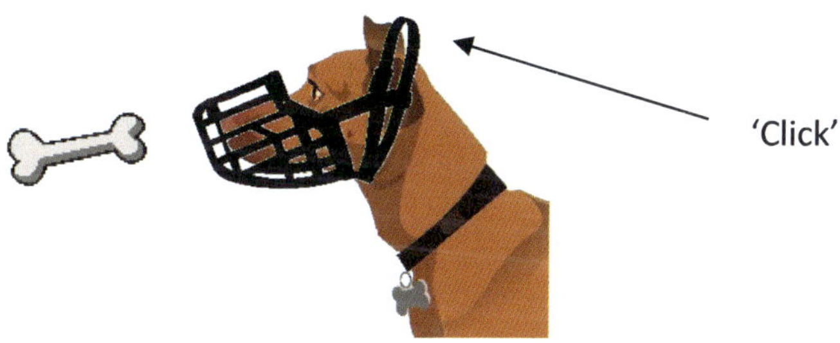

Step 7- Build the duration that the dog wears the muzzle before it is removed. Ensure you tailor this to the needs of the individual. Also add other commands (sit) in-between putting the muzzle on and off.

Dominance Theory Debunked

The common misunderstanding of dominance in pet dogs originated from a study in the 1970s revolving around a group of unrelated, captive wolves. The results from this study suggested the wolves were part of a strict hierarchy controlled by force and aggression.

The scientists who originally formed this theory have since understood that these unrelated, captive wolves behave far differently to those who roam freely in family groups. Therefore, these animals do not use aggression to gain status, so there is no reason we why should be using force and intimidation to train these animals and show them who is 'alpha'. However, dogs do have a hierarchy amongst one another but this is subtle and maintained without noticeable enforcement.

Training using forcing and intimidation creates a scared, timid, unpredictable dog which finds it difficult to learn and trust. Training using reward-based methods creates happy, puzzle solving family members.

Age at which Human and Dog Emotions Appear

Neuroscientists have found comparable evidence that adult dogs possess a level of awareness similar to that of a 2 ½ year old child. Therefore, we should be providing as much guidance and care for dogs as we would children of the same age. This shows that dogs do not develop the emotions of shame, pride, guilt and contempt.

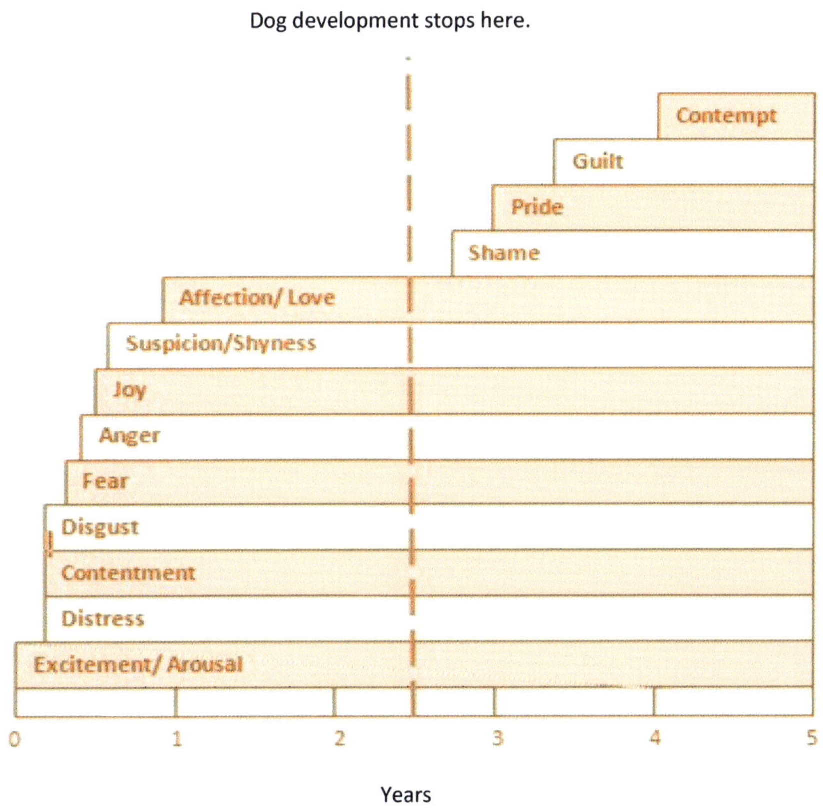

Source: Stanley Coren, Ph.D., 2013. Canine Corner. Psychology Today.

Choosing a Trainer

The dog training industry is not strictly regulated, so some may call themselves a dog trainer without being certified. Inexperienced or old fashioned trainers could cause or worsen behavioural problems, by using unkind or ineffective methods.

Check List:

- Ensure kind, modern and effective training methods are used without the use of pain or fear.
- Check the trainers are experienced, fully qualified and insured. UK organisations that attempt to regulate dog trainers, include the APDT, COAPE, APBC, ABTC, IMDT and TCBTS.
- Watch a class before you decide to take your dog and observe how the trainer handles problematic situations and clients.
- Ensure the syllabus meets your requirements and works towards your dog being a well-mannered canine citizen.
- Instead of 'quick fixes' that only suppress unwanted behaviour, ensure your dog is being provided with a positive outlet or coping strategies for their behaviour.
- Question what the trainer is doing and if you are uncomfortable with the way the dogs are being taught, protect your dog and leave.

The Author

I strive to continuously educate myself in the most up to date scientific research. It is still surprising how many trainers are working using old and detrimental methods. It soon shows that where knowledge ends, violence begins.

I gained a first class degree in Animal Behaviour and shortly after began working as the Dog Trainer and Behaviour Coordinator, at the National Animal Welfare Trust. I am a full member of the APDT, ABTC and provisional APBC, I have a soft spot for rescue dogs and strive for that light bulb moment when the dog realises what it needs to do.

Anyone that says they have a 'perfect' dog is fibbing and it is unacceptable and delusional to portray that dogs have to be perfectly behaved and bombproof. They are thinking, feeling creatures with a mind of their own. We can only guide them as best as we can with our current level of knowledge.

I run Suppawt, a bespoke, understanding and tailored training service. Specialising in Rescue dogs and those with reactivity.

www.suppawt.com

Testimonials from Industry Experts

I wish I had been given a book like that when I had my first rescue dog all those years ago. A great book, covers all the necessary stuff usually encountered by rescue owners etc., not too complicated, easy to read. Factual and not too overwhelming. - **Kay Attwood KCAI**

Here to stay is a great intro for people into the importance of understanding learning theory and relating it to their pet dogs. - **Karen Wild CCAB**

Hip, hip, hooray! If you've welcomed an adolescent or adult rescue dog into your life, this is the book you need. This is the best book on bringing home a rescue dog I've ever read. In fact, while the book is tailor made for rescue dogs, the information provided is useful for any dog, puppy or adult, newcomer or old-timer, equally. The presentation is quiet efficient and distilled into a palatable and relatable package. The text gets right down to the bare essentials to get you up and running training your dog as soon as possible. The techniques outlined are solid and science-based but manage to be user-friendly and the principles of effective behaviour change are beautifully explained in concise and clear terms. Ms. Clark has left no stones unturned and you'll find yourself referring to this helpful guide as you form your relationship with your new best friend. – **Kelly Gorman Dunbar (Open Paw Founder)**

Resources

My top 5 must read books:

The Human Half of Dog Training- Rise VanFleet

Good Little Dog Book- Ian Dunbar

Canine Body Language- Brenda Aloff

Click to Calm- Emma Parsons

Reaching the Animal Mind- Karen Pryor

Online Resources:

www.naturallyhappydogs.com

www.clickertraining.com

www.apdt.co.uk

www.apbc.org.uk

www.dogstardaily.com

Acknowledgements

Big thank you to the team at Cambridge Dogs, for tutoring me whilst I was at university. University alone would never have been enough to kick start my career.

Thank you to the team at NAWT Watford for supporting me and giving me the chance to see what I could do! This is where I took home my amazing lad Jasper and my girl Brie.

Thank you to my family and friends for your support. A special shout out to George Mickleburgh and Katie Fulcher for their continuous encouragement and Sally Marchant and Kevin Marchant for their ongoing support and doing 3 photo shoots until we were able to get the perfect picture.

Printed in Great Britain
by Amazon

59181358R00067